TANTRA
SEX FOR THE SOUL

TANTRA
SEX FOR THE SOUL

SOMANANDA MOSES MAIMON

Tantra: Sex for the Soul
Somananda Moses Maimon

Editor: Lori Doyle
Layout: Joel Tambaur
Cover Design: Lauri Tuulik
Photos: Private Collection

www.bhairavayoga.com
ISBN 978-9949-33-350-9

DEDICATION

I would like to dedicate this book to my
guru, Swami Vivekananda Saraswati,
who opened my eyes to the truth and
showed me the Absolute.

ACKNOWLEDGMENTS

I would like to acknowledge the following people:

Swami Vivekananda Saraswati, my guru,
who made me who I am today

Agama Yoga School of Tantra

Liisa Vask for her incredible support
and key advice in so many regards

Lori Doyle for an amazing job of editing
and help with preparation of the book

Tiina Ristimets, my publisher, for asking me
to write the book and bringing the project
to possibility with her support and expertise

Ingrid Peek for her creative input and wonderful mind

Katrin Oitra for her excellent work in the
transcription of my thoughts to paper

CONTENTS

About Bhairava Yoga

INTRODUCTION

When I first met my guru and teacher in India, I was looking to learn Yoga. I was fascinated by the Yoga tradition and the deep knowledge it contained. On the day we met, I walked into a Yoga hall in Rishikesh, India, listened to a lecture he gave, and I was amazed. I felt as if I had just been introduced to secrets I had been searching for my whole life.

My teacher was speaking about certain teachings from Yoga and then he began talking about Tantra. That was the first time I had ever been exposed to Tantra and its hidden meanings. Step by step and month by month, my teacher took me through the teachings of Tantra and revealed the secrets that this supreme spiritual system has to share. It was a revelation that would have a huge impact on my life from then on.

In the years to come I became a tantric man myself and a teacher of Tantra. I saw how the knowledge of Tantra had the potential to change people's lives for the better and to bestow remarkable benefits.

Tantra is an ancient science that includes a complete understanding of the universe and reality. It is a path of evolution and, therefore, includes within its lore a wide variety of different aspects, from diet to energy, from metaphysics to daily applications, from astronomy and astrology to the use of colors and sounds, from *mantras* and cosmic powers to sexuality and true love.

It is, in my humble opinion, the most valuable and comprehensive science humanity has ever known. For centuries and even millennia, it has been kept more or less secret, yet in the last few decades it has become more accessible to those fortunate to find authentic teachings and to realize their amazing value and potential.

In this book, I chose to focus mostly on the sexual teachings of Tantra. In my experience as a Tantra teacher, I have found that most people respond very directly and powerfully to the tantric sexual teachings. As for the metaphysical, philosophical, meditative, and purely yogic aspects of Tantra, as much as they are superior to any other system – powerful and awe-inspiring – those aspects are less accessible for the average tantric enthusiast.

Moreover, the sexual teachings of Tantra are very urgently needed in our modern society, in which so many couples and individuals are seeking meaningful sexuality and relationships, as well as a way to reach a deeper connection with each other. Thus, I have found that the tantric sexual teachings are a blessing to nearly all seekers, having brought great transformation and fulfillment to many.

Therefore, in this book, you will find references to the more esoteric elements of the tantric teachings but the focus will always remain on the sexual aspects in order to bring the maximum benefits to readers.

Let the tantric adventure begin!

I

THE ORIGINS OF TANTRA / WHAT IS TANTRA?

Tantra is a vast metaphysical system, unrelated to any religion, which originated in India and Tibet many centuries ago. This very scientific, comprehensive system gives the human being a gateway into the structure of reality and a practical understanding of the basic laws of the universe, in essence providing us the bases for development as human beings. First and foremost, Tantra is a path to spiritual evolution.

The ancient origins of Tantra can be traced to certain texts which are called the *agamas*. These texts, some of which have not yet been translated into modern languages, encompass teachings on an enormous variety of subjects. To an uninitiated person, the information seems too vast, of studies possibly not even related or contradictory. What does architecture have to do with sex or healing or rituals or astrology? The *agamas* covered these topics and many more. From the practical to the metaphysical, Tantra has something to say about everything, because ultimately all of these subjects are related in a spiritual worldview. In fact, the definition of Tantra is: a web of interconnection.

BASIC PRINCIPLES OF TANTRA

It is important to begin with a solid foundation of understanding about Tantra so that one can develop the tools to bring philosophical theory into tangible reality in daily experience.

In Sanskrit the word Tantra is translated as the "warp" of a loom – that which weaves everything together into a net of connections. Tantra is a science of correlations which reveals to us that the universe is holographic in nature. Everything is reflected in everything else, the universal Macrocosm can be found in the individual microcosm. Not only is there a cosmic revelation in even the smallest of all of creation, there is also a seemingly unfathomable interconnection between every single thing in the universe and everything else. The Sufis say that when you cut a blade of grass, you impact the galaxies – the blade of grass and galaxies have an interconnection. You may have heard of this idea, illustrated in the "butterfly effect," that a butterfly flapping its wings in a tropical rainforest is causally intertwined with a tsunami somewhere on the other side of the planet in an invisible network of energy. Tantra is training in recognizing the subtleties of these connections. When you tune your perception into this level of reality, you will begin to understand this idea at the deepest level of your own being.

In every atom there are worlds within worlds.
— Yogavasistha

The first and most important concept of Tantra is Shakti, which translates as energy, yet also means power and goddess. The whole of universal manifestation is energy, Shakti. However, energy is not singular and it does not exist apart from what we can deem to be *consciousness* – thus the duality, or polarity, of Shiva and Shakti.

While these terms are found in the Hindu tradition, they represent far more than a mythological or metaphorical understanding referring to human-like paganistic gods or goddesses. They in fact represent the exact metaphysical nature of reality in the tantric tradition.

The polarity of Shiva and Shakti is the relationship between the two aspects of reality: the unmanifested (or mysterious and undifferentiated) and manifested (everything we see, feel, touch, or essentially everything our universe includes, otherwise known as energy or Shakti). The unmanifested, known as *purusha* in Tantra, is beyond manifestation or reality as we know it, *prakriti*. This unmanifested reality, also known as Shiva, cannot really be put into words, and therefore we can simply call it the Absolute.

The Goddess resides in all women and the Lord abides in all men.
— Jvalavali Vajramala

Tantra is the understanding that everything is connected to everything else in our reality. This approach, as a science of correlations, is found in many other spiritual teachings and, not surprisingly, it has been corroborated by modern science. Scientists of the last hundred years reached similar conclusions, most prominently noted in the fields of quantum mechanics and quantum physics, which demonstrated to us that everything is energy and has no independent reality apart from consciousness. Reality is energy. For example, in the now-discredited way of looking at the structure of the atom from decades ago, a nucleus had electrons revolving around it. In quantum physics and other modern research, atomic distances are incredibly vast, proportionately speaking similar to the distances found in our solar system. Where do you find the electron? You don't. It is both a wave and a particle, as well as an electron. When does it flip? Where?

We can also reference Schrödinger's cat, which demonstrated the quantum theory of multiple realities (superposition). We're talking about something real here – this is not fantasy. Atoms do flicker in and out of reality when consciousness is involved. So what does this say about our universe?

Modern science, especially quantum physics, has confirmed what tantrics said thousands of years ago, that reality is energy. If **everything is energy**, everything is Shakti. Most religions try to tell us that this reality is actually on one level an experiment – we are here to be tested, to purify our souls, and then eventually we reach the kingdom of heaven or *nirvana* or any of the myriad names given to the "realm beyond." In these ascetic religious views, when you reach there, you then discover the truth which renders this reality here now on Earth, this labyrinth, useless.

But Tantra disputes this worldview. The whole point in Tantra is that this reality has value – this reality is a divine realm on its own, reflecting the sacred, holy essence of that which created it. And that makes all the difference. It means that this reality is made of energy, which is called Shakti, the Goddess. It means that there is a God, the unmanifested aspect of the universe, Shiva.

> *The union of man and woman is like the mating*
> *of Heaven and Earth. It is because of their correct mating*
> *that Heaven and Earth last forever. Humans have*
> *lost this secret and have therefore become mortal.*
> *By knowing it the Path to Immortality is opened.*
> — Shang-Ku-San-Tai

This is where Tantra arrives at a very practical approach. It says that since everything is energy and energy follows special types of rules, you can scientifically predict certain things. And if we have rules that cover all kinds of energy? We can control energy. And if the whole universe is energy, we can control the universe. The tantrics considered it important to understand that reality is energy and that we are part of it, which takes us directly to Tantra's very practical applications in all facets of our lives. Tantra says that if everything is energy, let's use this energy. Everything is relevant because by virtue of an energetic definition, everything is connected to everything.

There is a very important common denominator to all of this – the teachings of Tantra resemble a somewhat shamanic approach to life. While in shamanism practitioners reach altered states of consciousness in order to encounter and interact with the spirit world, we do not here refer to shamanism in any forest-dwelling, primitive sense. In this case, we refer to a metaphysical sensibility denoting a spiritual approach to life, a spiritual animation of that which seems mundane. If you compared this to Christianity or Buddhism or any other religion or spiritual path, Tantra also addresses reality. It helps us understand the real nature of existence and to identify our purpose in life. It ignores financial questions in favor of the destiny of the soul, why we are here. These are existential, metaphysical questions. Many people caught up in materialistic life consider these concerns irrelevant. Even in an academic environment, Tantra's attention to energy is considered akin to the paganistic naming of natural forces, etc., as if a materialistic view supersedes Tantra in spiritual maturity, which is an ignorant perception. The ancient tantrics handed down the teachings of great masters who had reached very high states of consciousness. And those masters concluded that *not* asking these fundamental questions was, in fact, the biggest mistake.

Tantra says that as human beings we all have a spark inside of us – *atman*, the divine essence that dwells within. This is our true nature. And understanding our true nature – seeking to know it with clarity and depth, existentially realizing it and not just intellectually discussing it as philosophy – is the nature of spiritual development. It is the nature of enlightenment.

> *There is a bridge between time and eternity;*
> *this bridge is the individual soul, the* jiva.
> *— Chandogya Upanishad*

TANTRA IS A TREASURE

The world is full of misunderstandings when it comes to Tantra. In the West, Tantra is commonly perceived as just an exotic – or wild and kinky – approach to sex. Unfortunately, this often remains the main focus, which displays a very limited understanding. There is so much more to it! The sexual components of Tantra represent only 5 to 10 percent of the tantric teachings. The rest includes a vast canon of tantric studies in science, the arts, aesthetics, healing, energy, *kundalini, Hatha Yoga*, other aspects of daily life, and of course rich spiritual traditions. Bookstores nowadays are full of books about Tantra, massage, sensuality training, and sexual positions, featuring many images suggesting a spiced-up, multiorgasmic sex life. This "pop culture" version of Tantra is an almost cartoonish and often very inaccurate representation. Although plenty of people try, learning Tantra from books – especially drawing from the very small selection of authentic guides available today – is still nothing compared to study with real masters, whether they are from India, Thailand, Europe, or anywhere else.

When Western travelers first visited India hundreds of years ago, due to their religious backgrounds, sex for them often involved much guilt and shame. Many religious Westerners would have sex maybe 10 times per year – therefore, the discovery of Tantra in India was obviously challenging. In comparison, people today may have sex 10 times a week, in which case Tantra can be a lifesaver. Tantra's rich spiritual legacy **helps modern people approach sexuality in a mature way**. It can help both us and our partners develop in terms of character, depth and tonus of personality, psychology, emotions, mental life, and spiritual evolution, reaching high states of consciousness. Our sexuality can represent the way our whole life grows as a fertile tree. Thus, even if you are a scientist or businessperson, Tantra can also do amazing things for you and help you achieve success in your profession.

You may ask how this is possible. As mentioned already, **one of the main principles of Tantra is that everything is connected to everything** in a science of correlations. **In addition, sex is connected to everything**. We might not see the connection but it is there. So if you have sex in the right way and channel your energies properly, whatever you do will be changed for the better. **Your approach to reality changes your reality.**

As previously explained, **Tantra says the universe and everything in it is energy** – from physical matter to emotions to intelligence to every aspect of all the comprehensible elements in our reality. Tantra also takes the science of energies even further. If we understand the universe, we understand ourselves. "Know thyself; then thou shalt know the universe and God," said Greek philosopher Pythagoras. Once we understand energy, despite its different faces, we find we can control ourselves and the environment much better. According to the **yogic logic** – the law of correspondence – the human being and the universe are identical, with the human being a miniature copy. According to the law of resonance, the frequency of energy triggers vibrational similitude, which means that two seemingly distinct objects will suddenly vibrate in the same manner, communing with one another. That is the essence of tantric practice: training our ability to attune ourselves to beneficial, harmonious energies or any energy we choose. If we can attune ourselves properly, we can "download" access to limitless sources of energy. Any type of energy can be amplified. **An infinity of energies waits at our fingertips!**

By following the tantric recipe, success is guaranteed. Love as a state of mind and not mere emotion can be reached. The ultimate goal of tantrics, for those who have the dedication to go all the way to the pinnacle of this process, is the evolution of true love, from one partner to another, from one transpersonally to humanity, a bridge created from the love toward the divine. If this state is reached, a human being is on his or her way to self-realization – demonstrating that through sexuality and love we can reach the same heights as all other religious practices – enlightenment, *nirvana*. Tantric practice, however, is not for everyone. In helping to improve the quality of our relationships, it is for everyone, yes. But taking it all the way to the highest spheres – this is not for everyone.

Life without love is like a tree without blossoms or fruit.
Love has no other desire but to fulfill itself. To melt and be like a
running brook that sings its melody to the night. To wake at dawn
with a winged heart and give thanks for another day of loving.
— Kahlil Gibran, *The Prophet*

The practice of Tantra is a rarity in the world. On top of that, authentic teachers are in addition scarce, an inherent difficulty faces practitioners in a world becoming more and more materially oriented, and the fact that Tantra takes courage and a certain "warrior's attitude" means that now, more than at other times in the history of our planet, it will take diligence to succeed in Tantra.

The original and ancient texts of Tantra commented in detail about the era in which we live – and these were texts written centuries and millennia ago. These texts explain how the ages, the cosmic cycles or *yugas*, flow in the universe. The tantrics say that there have been great civilizations on this planet before us and many secrets are not known because they remain lost in time or hidden. According to Tantra, there have been four cycles of approximately 6,400 years each, which contribute to one big cycle lasting about 25,000 years. Each of these smaller cycles represents different souls who live (or have lived) on this planet. The *yugas* have been defined in Tantra with specific names, namely *Satya*, *Treta*, *Dvapara*, and *Kali*. In the Greek tradition, they are known as, respectively, the Golden, Silver, Bronze, and Iron Ages. The spiritual frequency of the *yugas* oscillates between very high in the *Satya Yuga* and very low in *Kali Yuga* – the fourth and last cycle in which we live today. These eras repeat in cycles, and soon *Satya Yuga* will begin again. *Kali Yuga*, as the last cycle, is deemed the lowest spiritually, which means that it is much more difficult for people in these times to make the spiritual efforts necessary to change their lives. Very few can do it. Only those who hear the inner calling, whose souls are their priorities, and who are prepared to dedicate themselves to spiritual efforts will really succeed in Tantra.

II

MY STORY

From a young age, I was attracted to knowledge about the powers of the mind, endlessly fascinated by accounts of people with paranormal abilities, stories about magic, and fields involving apparently superhuman strength, such as martial arts. In my early teens, with great enthusiasm I began studying martial arts, specifically karate, and I enjoyed it very much. By my late teens I was obligated to serve three years in the Israeli Army, after which I pursued a university degree in law and eventually became an attorney. Throughout these years, I had very little time to devote to my passions.

For several years I practiced law. At some point the universe brought me back on track in the oddest way; my father became sick with a severe illness and I immediately decided that I wanted to help him. Accompanying him on all his doctors' visits, going through the process of trying to become well, I understood that Western medicine had little to offer and all scenarios seemed grim. I refused to believe there were no credible options and decided to do my own research into alternative healing, various Eastern traditions, etc. I was in my mid-20s and, at some point, after all kinds of study and research, I stumbled upon a book about Yoga by Yesudian Selvarajan, *Yoga and Health*. It rang a bell in my soul. Like everything, I tested it on myself, beginning a *Hatha Yoga* practice. Immediately I felt Yoga was very special and I tried to introduce it to my father, but he was not interested. Despite this, I felt a deep connection with Yoga nonetheless, and I continued in my practice.

My father's illness was serious and I was very persistent in trying to help him heal. I experimented with all kinds of things – some he agreed to try and some he didn't, due to stubbornness or inertia. At one point he seemed to be on the road to restored health, and I took this opportunity to explore what had been a recent turning point in my life: the discovery of Yoga. After reading that first book, I did more research, stumbled upon more books, and dove into them hungrily, with an aspiration that fed my neglected soul. My interest in Yoga grew much deeper, and at some point I realized that it had become so powerful to me that I needed to start taking courses. So even though at this time I was putting in long days at work, I went to Yoga classes in the evening instead of going home to rest.

HOW I FOUND MY TEACHER

All the ancient texts I read echoed the same caveat: It is essential to find the right teacher. At some point I realized I had to do just that. In 1999 I sold my car, completed my employment contract, moved my belongings to a family member's house, bought a backpack, and went to India. My wish was to see other countries, too, as I had not traveled much.

While I was in India, I was looking for someone who would teach me Yoga. I followed a journey like that of many Westerners on a similar quest in India; I visited all kinds of ashrams, met various Yoga teachers, and became confused, because so many of them were not genuine. Indians understand that Westerners will pay a pretty penny for Yoga, so every Tom, Dick, and Harry will try to sell it to you, without actually having the knowledge. They figure (correctly) that most people will take them at face value and will not investigate their credentials or have the wisdom to verify their authenticity or teachings.

Human unhappiness results from mankind's acceptance
of the lowest conditions of our minds. By the practice
of Yoga, all such conditioning can be overcome.
— Patanjali's *Yoga Sutras*

But I knew what I was looking for and, in 1999, I found myself in Rishikesh – known affectionately as the "world capital of Yoga," a holy town in the northern Himalayas situated on the Ganges River. In a short time, I met my guru, Swami Vivekananda Saraswati. (On a side note: A "guru" is a teacher who helps point out where your ego is refusing to transform once you have committed to spiritual practice. This teacher is someone whose wisdom is verified, whose discrimination is solid, and in whom you can surrender your trust. That teacher is called a guru in spiritual traditions of initiation such as Tantra. However, since the meaning of this word has been at times debased and discredited through misunderstandings and nonspiritual cults which borrowed this word, I will use teacher throughout this book.)

As I listened to him, within a matter of 20 minutes, I understood that I had found exactly what I was looking for. Surprisingly, he was not an Indian person – he was from Romania, in fact – but I knew he was the real thing. I started studying and practicing with him and the results came almost immediately. I felt inspired and full of enthusiasm the more I progressed, and the more I practiced and studied, the more the benefits of Yoga were revealed to me. I stayed there for six months and did not want to leave. However, eventually, due to pressure from my traveling companion at the time, I reluctantly left, promising to return quickly.

The following months were filled with travels to Thailand, Japan, and New Zealand, after which I returned to Israel where my father had turned back to his old ways and was already navigating the last stages of his illness. I stayed close by and supported him, but by then it was too late for him to recover and he soon passed away.

For me, my father's passing was a very contemplative occasion, because we had shared a tight bond in life, always close. I took time to mourn his passing and to quietly grieve. As soon as I felt this cycle to be complete, I returned to India, where I rejoined my teacher and resumed my Yoga studies and training.

My teacher, Swami, as he is lovingly known, taught mostly tantric Yoga, which I had been exposed to since the first stages of my Yoga studies. I had already known I wanted to teach this when I first came upon it the year prior, and he had confirmed my fitness and aptitude for Tantra and teaching Yoga before I had left on my travels.

Since Swami himself had to leave for a short visit to Thailand to renew his visa, he took a look at me and asked me to give lessons in his place. He told me: You are ready to teach and I can support you. I was a bit doubtful, as it sounded almost mystical – how would he "support" me? Through energy conveyed telepathically? I hadn't taken any notes, I had no materials, and generally I felt unprepared. But he smiled confidently and said: You are ready. And I trusted him.

The hour of my first lesson arrived. I had made some notes and started giving the lecture. Suddenly I felt the information flying through me, like a higher power was guiding me. I felt the sense of an empowerment to teach bestowed upon me by my teacher. After my first – and very successful – lecture, I did what Swami would usually do and asked the class if anybody had questions. When the mostly Westerners asked questions, I felt like a beginner who at first recognized he did not have the answers, but when my mouth opened, the answers came out! I was truly amazed. I felt my teacher's presence, felt him speaking through me, felt his personality and spirit literally inside me. I was almost like an observer from the outside – I myself was interested in the answers that came from my own mouth, as if I were also a student listening. This experience has continued ever since; I feel my teacher's presence with me whenever I teach.

In the years that followed, I realized that I was blessed to have had such an enfoldment of events. The manner in which I found my teacher felt like it had been a divinely orchestrated synchronicity. Finding the right teacher is essential and, to this end, I have developed my recommendations in this regard as part of the last chapter of this book, Tantric Spirituality.

THE BEGINNING OF TANTRIC TIMES

As I continued my studies in India, my development in Yoga and Tantra grew deeper and I began to explore my interest in sexual Tantra. I had realized they were not separate systems, but rather fully integrated into each other. My training in sexual Tantra revealed to me another great surprise.

My tantric practices at the sexual level with various partners quickly led me to realize that I had a talent in this. I was meeting success easily, able to experience sexuality in a different way. It was no longer a wild blur of mere passionate encounters. Instead, lovemaking became a slow, powerful, far more deep and satisfying connection with my partner. I noticed suddenly that my pleasure was under my control. I could prolong, enhance, and deepen it almost without limits. I was also amazed to see the effects of my practice in action with my partners, because at this time I did not have one steady partner.

I began to truly understand female sexuality. I had always perceived women's pleasure as something mysterious – I knew they could have fun, make some sounds, and their bodies would respond in various ways. I perceived all these signals during a sexual union. I also remembered the most basic thing women aspired for before Tantra: Let's wait for each other so we can come together. Ten or 20 seconds of coming together with a partner was a big deal back then, but this is child's play compared to what Tantra can do for men and women individually and in couples.

A woman's body can respond sexually at a much deeper level, sustaining sexual pleasure far longer than I had ever realized. I enjoyed the beauty of being able to continuously increase and tease the pleasure into an almost infinite existence. I discovered that orgasm can be a more profound experience. Instead of representing an "explosion," it can be almost a self-sustained, continuous wave of pleasure which can be explored and enjoyed for longer and longer periods of time.

Later on in my tantric training, I developed far beyond the sexual aspects. I discovered the secret teachings of sound, color, the *Maha Vidya* cosmic powers, and other facets of Tantra which cannot be revealed. I continued my teachings with my teacher for three and a half years, with short breaks to visit family and work, in order to save up some money.

By this time, 2003, I had become one of Swami's main teachers and he recommended that I open a branch of our school, Agama Yoga, in Israel, and I did. After a few months I left my Israeli group with other teachers and joined Swami in Thailand because our headquarters had moved there, where it remains today. I continued my education in Yoga and Tantra and did a great deal of teaching.

In Thailand my training deepened significantly, and I began a special individualized program to develop the chakras, which is a part of the tantric curriculum. As a result of this *sadhana*, I went on a journey with many upheavals and a concerted transformation of the ego, which is also part of the tantric process.

TAMING THE WILD BEAST OF SEXUAL ENERGY

At one point in my life Tantra brought me into a process of growth, where I was confronted by my own practice. I was challenged by the limitations, ugly sides of the ego, and lower aspects of the mind that manifested sexually through relationships, mistakes in tantric relationships, and learning how to take a relationship from a multiorgasmic level to a spiritually mature and profound level.

This is a very difficult phase that can take years but eventually leads to self-transformation and self-evolution. It was not at all easy. I remember moments when I was amazed how low I could feel and how difficult the challenges could be when struggling with the ego. Sometimes the solution was indeed so easy, but the ego would not allow it. In Tantra the challenge is much more real than in other spiritual teachings where the ego is also present but is not confronted. Tantra is often described as riding a wild dragon – learning how to control the basic, animal nature of the human being.

While through my tantric training I had learned about the concept of open relationships, I also realized that in Tantra this remains a personal choice and is not an obligation. Some find it very appealing to experience multiple relationships, which can help us learn to confront the ego and lower emotions, and learn to control these aspects of ourselves. And some like to experience Tantra in one-on-one relationships.

I decided to head down the more difficult path – exploring open relationships. The confrontation with the ego is relentless and vehement. You realize the ugly face of jealousy and possessiveness head on, and just when you think you have overcome it, it comes back. You have to keep challenging yourself on that level and vow not to rest until you've actualized a real change in your behavior and awareness. Running away from the problem does not help and is, in fact, not a tantric attitude. Tantra advises that we not skirt around the obstacles on our path in fear and avoidance, but rather move toward them with courage and determination.

Practicing Tantra, Yoga, and meditation, I explored the options of an open relationship. What helped with the ego was the practice itself – *Kundalini Yoga* and high-level Kashmiri Shaivism techniques that are not taught to beginners. Soon I started to see the changes and transformation taking place. Transformation with spiritual practice is usually very subtle, taking months and years, and a practitioner feels subjectively that nothing is happening. In such cases, only those who haven't seen you in years could say: Wow, you have changed a lot. It is difficult to see when you yourself are part of the process.

Every yogi and tantric practitioner follows their practice and techniques on a daily basis and their growth continues all the time. In August, 2008, I came to the most important moment in my spiritual evolution when – thanks to the grace of my teacher and with his guidance – I reached some form of spiritual realization. From that point on, the growth took an even higher form and I began to teach in Europe, with the guidance of my teacher, presenting Tantra workshops, holding retreats, and giving teachings in countries such as Hungary, Holland, Germany, England, Israel, France, and Estonia.

In 2009 I visited Estonia for the first time and fell completely in love with the country and people. I was invited back repeatedly to do more workshops and I returned each time with joy. Early in 2010 I made the conscious decision to move permanently to Estonia, becoming a resident and opening Bhairava Yoga, a branch of my Yoga school, in Tallinn.

Bhairava is one of the names of Lord Shiva representing his frightening manifestation, which is associated with annihilation. This is not Shiva from the Indian pantheon, but Shiva from *Kundalini Yoga* and the understandings of Kashmiri Shaivism, one of the most advanced tantric lineages in the history of mankind. In these spiritual teachings and philosophy, Shiva is perceived as the divine source of all tantric knowledge and the nondualistic essence of all things manifested and unmanifested. In his aspect as Bhairava, Shiva annihilates the ego and all low things, bringing a human-being to a spiritual state.

Since I follow the teachings of Kashmiri Shaivism, I chose this name because it fits my mentality and yogic style. In the Estonian school I hold Yoga courses, present many types of Yoga-related workshops, and we additionally host many meditation retreats, events, and other activities. More than 3,000 people have participated in my workshops or joined the Yoga courses in Estonia. I still teach in Thailand, India, and Europe, but I am currently much more focused in Estonia.

Following my spiritual realizations in 2008, which have been reinforced by the repeated spiritually high states I've continued to experience until today, I've decided to dedicate myself to giving these teachings and spreading this tantric message as widely as possible. I have seen both in my own development and transformation and also in many others that Tantra can be a blessing that affects all people very positively in their day-to-day lives, bringing balance and helping psychologically and spiritually. That is why I am determined to share this knowledge and feel blessed to do so.

III

ENERGY IS THE KEY

Most religions teach us one simple message: Life is an elaborate illusion. We should ignore it and focus on consciousness, focus on escaping this reality which imprisons us. It is their way of looking at it and it is true, in such a context. Buddha said that this reality is suffering; one has to reach *nirvana* to find the way out of the suffering. It may sound like a negative approach but it is true – life is what you make of it. If you see it as a prison, then it becomes your prison.

Tantra suggests that we think of energy as something divine. Consider it as a goddess that can be worshipped, and in so doing that goddess loves us back, grants us favors and gifts, and guides our path in life. As a result of this much more positive approach, we learn about this reality and can surpass it. This tantric way is much more efficient and powerful than any other approach.

THE MOST POWERFUL ENERGY – OUR DRIVING FORCE

Tantra has an extraordinary and unique view of human sexuality. It says that of all the energies in nature in this reality, there is one type of energy that is the most fundamental and powerful – the sexual energy. Why? Because the sexual energy can do something remarkable – it can create life! It is also true that modern science can create life using artificial insemination, but even then on an elementary level, the sexual connection is there. Even if only semen and an egg exist in a test tube, this still represents the sexual union at a cellular level. At every level of the universe we see the sexual energy, the polarity, the dance between plus and minus, male and female, yin and yang, from the smallest atoms and amoebae to the highest life forms. In the human being sexual energy has a starring role. Not only is it the energy used for procreation, but it is an energy that affects us in many other dimensions.

As a result, sexual energy is like magic. It can create life and bring consciousness to a path of expression. Understanding this, the tantrics recognized the powerful potential of the sexual energy – it is the spark of life. This energy we are all born with is called in Tantra and Yoga by name *ojas*. It means the sexual energy, the life force inherent in all of us, each man and woman. It is possible to learn to use that creative potential inside us.

Tantra says that the whole universe is energy, Shakti, but of all energies the sexual energy is the most basic, most important, and most prevalent. All animals have the sexual urge – none of them is impervious to sex. Even at the level of the atom, we find a form of attraction between electrons and protons. In their deep meditation, tantrics understood that the whole universe is sexual, but not in our common way of thinking. It is very important to differentiate! The sexual energy that manifests in the human being is actually a spiritual desire based deep within us. This most fundamental desire has sown in us a longing for union. We need to unite the microcosm of our being with the Macrocosm, the cosmos. Yoga means union in Sanskrit. **In the lower levels of the human being, fervor and the need to find God manifest in the sexual energy**. So putting it bluntly, we could say: The hornier you are, the more spiritual you are. It is a road that can lead us higher. Here, it is important to explain that the sexual desire is only one indication of a deep spiritual force. For some people the spiritual impulse is strong but may not manifest as a sexual urge. Also, when reaching the highest levels, this spiritual impulse is no longer related to sexuality and becomes more pure and elevated.

A KEY TO UNLOCK EVERYTHING INSIDE US?

We were not given the gift of sexual energy merely to procreate. According to Tantra we can learn to develop and use this powerful energy, to channel it in our bodies properly, using it to ignite our aspiration and take us further to new dimensions of discovery in the realm of human potential. Tantra believes that this energy is the key that unlocks the divine secrets inside us. **The nature of sexual energy is that of a force under pressure**.

For example, if we look at young people who just hit puberty, what do we see? They are usually restless and full of energy, wanting to do all kinds of crazy things. Some may say that's just the sign of silly youth. However, this is not necessarily the case! Young people are boiling inside and, as we know, extremely horny. As we grow older something changes. According to yogis and tantrics we do not simply grow older physically, but in fact with time we lose more and more of our sexual energy. When we lose it, our internal pressure declines dramatically and all that beautiful madness we had when we were young starts becoming flat. With that, our success in meditation and spirituality diminishes as well.

Yogis compare sexual pressure to the mechanism of a steam engine, which powered trains in the olden days. It works like this: You have a big boiler full of water, you light a fire underneath which boils the water and turns it into steam, creating intense pressure. That pressure generates the enormous energy needed to create the mechanical movement propelling the locomotive to haul tons of weight and move very fast. How do you stop the steam engine? It is very easy: You pull the lever and release the pressure. And then the powerful train, which was churning rapidly along, stops on a dime. The energy vanishes when the pressure is released.

When I refer to *ojas* as the sexual energy, people might commonly infer an interpretation along the lines of sexual urges or hunger. But this is not the true meaning of *ojas*. In the tantric environment as well as that of Chinese Taoism, the *ojas* is a limited amount of extremely potent energy which manifests as sexual energy but is also the energy in the substratum of the human being. It's the essential energy, the essence behind all other energies, the essential motivator of the human being. Tantra quantifies that energy as consisting of three and a half drops in the base of the spine, located somewhere in the area of the root chakra. But don't let this quantification fool you – these are not drops measurable as a liquid. The *ojas* can be considered perhaps something like highly condensed atomic energy which has the capability to create life when used for procreation and, if used in the tantric sense for spiritual purposes, may bring about spiritual evolution with correct practice.

Ojas is finite and its loss will cost you physically. When you are born, this energy associated with the life force is at full capacity – like a full battery. Slowly over our lifetimes, through the range of manners in which we deplete this energy, our batteries drain…. But there is no recharger for the *ojas*. The sexual energy cannot be recovered; once lost, it's gone. The more of it we lose, the more we will begin to notice increasing weakness, the appearance of degenerative conditions and diseases, and the manifestation of physical problems, including the early symptoms of aging and even premature death – all as a result of the abuse and loss of the *ojas*.

In the positive sense, the *ojas* or sexual energy is our driving force. In the tantric and yogic traditions, the method for controlling and stabilizing the sexual energy is called *brahmacharya*. Interestingly, when we look at older religions and spiritual teachings, all of them had something to say about sex. If sex is so irrelevant why did all religions talk about it, and usually quite negatively? "Don't do it... it is the original sin... you will go to hell... you are an animalistic person and the devil is waiting for you... just don't do it!" Why was there such a big agenda with sex?

The tantric answer would be that this preoccupation did not concern the sexual act itself. While religions have not recognized *ojas* in the same way as we do in Tantra, their objectives rely on its conservation. We can say that religions share certain objectives for their followers: keeping the human being enthusiastic, motivated, and full of zeal for spirituality, progress, bettering one's life, and other spiritual ideals – in one form or another, communion with God or a higher purpose. But obviously, religious founders and leaders have seen that when a person engages in sex (and according to Tantra, loses *ojas*), there is a steep decline in motivation and enthusiasm, and even faith may start flagging. The zeal for God simply diminishes.

From a tantric viewpoint, what happens to us when this pressure declines? Physically, our muscles and brains don't start to atrophy. However, we may suddenly notice energetic changes that filter into our beings. The sexual energy, the *ojas*, as the energy that underlies all other energies, represents the pressure. And when the pressure decreases, something in us is somehow reduced – our creativity, efficiency, and intensity. Look at teenagers and young adults who are full of energy and the will to change the world... and then ask them 20 years later about how their world-changing plans went. Quite often you'll get the answer: "Oh, it didn't work out, and I got busy with other things." You can see in this person a defeated attitude, a loss of drive, reduced energy and personal force. On some level there is more lethargy and less creativity, and the attention turns toward worldly satisfactions. These are all manifestations of a state in which *ojas* which has dwindled away. Sexual energy is behind our spiritual aspiration. It is what leads us to think about God, liberation, and enlightenment, what drives us to find meaning in this universe, in life, and in everything we do.

According to Tantra, the problem in the "*ojas* dilemma" is not sex itself, but the loss of sexual energy during non-tantric sex. In the average non-tantric sexual liaison, a man's ejaculation and a woman's explosive orgasm lead to a loss of this *ojas* Shakti. The mechanisms that explain exactly how the ejaculation or, in the case of women, the explosive orgasm and menstruation disturb the economy of *ojas* in the body will be explained in future books. But for now, suffice it to say that non-tantric sex dramatically taxes the essence of life, *ojas*.

A man should learn to control his ejaculation. To be greedy for feminine beauty and emit beyond one's vigor injures every vein, nerve, and organ in the body, and gives rise to every illness. Correct practice of sexual intercourse can cure every ailment and at the same time open the doors to Liberation.
— Yang-Sheng-Yao-Chi

TWO OPTIONS FOR CONSERVING SEXUAL ENERGY

All religions have noted this phenomenon that occurs with our loss of *ojas*, energy, through non-tantric sex – that the more we lose, the more our spiritual impulse dissipates. We may go to church, meditate, or do any other spiritual practice and yet we will sit there and achieve zero results. Why? Because without sexual energy under pressure the "steam engine" doesn't work.

This principle of conserving the *ojas* is presented in the classic Yoga teachings of India under the term *brahmacharya*. *Brahmacharya* is a Sanskrit word belonging to the *yamas* and *niyamas* of Yoga and it literally translates into control over the sexual energy. Brahma relates to the creative potential in the human being, or the sexual energy, and *acharya* means to stabilize, make firm, control. Thus *brahmacharya* means complete control over the sexual energy or, in other words, no loss of sexual energy whatsoever. This is a very important principle on any spiritual path, including Tantra. Therefore, we must always remember that there is no Tantra without *brahmacharya*.

The solution to this problem of lost vital energy over time has always been found in one of two options: the primitive direct solution or the more sophisticated solution. The primitive solution is obvious: We can practice celibacy, which means not having sex with ourselves or others, and then our pressure is in its mode of full power. In this state, we meditate, make great progress in our spiritual practice, and move to the next level. The pressure is the secret of success. And in most spiritual paths this ascetic, direct solution of abstinence has been prescribed. In tandem, they expound colorful and frightening stories of sins which are punished by suffering. As religions offer exoteric teachings, thus taking an outer circle approach (whereas esoteric traditions cultivate an inner circle), they sponsor teachings for the masses so that anyone can relate to it. Let me pause to clarify here that I believe religion can create a lot of good for those who are helped by it, and by no means do I oppose it.

The primitive solution is very powerful. Millions on the planet – from nuns and monks to yogis and many others – have chosen this path of celibacy. However, for the average person living in modern times, a life without sex is simply not acceptable – we would not choose to give up this wonderful aspect of life. And that's where Tantra comes in, with the sophisticated option. What if we could learn a type of sexuality in which we don't lose the *ojas* and can still experience the beauty of lovemaking? Would that still be considered *brahmacharya* or, in other words, continence? Tantra reveals that it is indeed possible and this path opens the door to something completely amazing. It is a spiritual path.

It is worth mentioning at this point that men and women lose *ojas* differently as a result of their different anatomies. Men's loss of *ojas* comes with the ejaculation and women's loss of *ojas* results primarily from having external and explosive, discharging orgasms, abundant menstruation, and childbirth. Other factors exist as well, which will be discussed at another time.

IMPLOSION VS. EXPLOSION

The tantrics discovered that by having sex in the tantric way – the sophisticated option number two – we don't lose our sexual energy. And when the pressure builds up, it brings both men and woman intense pleasure. One big problem nowadays is that, after an orgasm, men are not full of energy but rather the opposite – they collapse and fall asleep. However, one of the most important things the tantrics discovered was that there does not have to be a loss of *ojas* with orgasm.

Lovemaking does not have to stop with an explosive orgasm. It can become very tender and become a much deeper experience and, when the pleasure increases, both men and women can discover that they are multiorgasmic. It is possible to have orgasms which last for a much longer period of time, leading to an experience of the profound side effects of lovemaking, such as higher states of consciousness.

If one should resolve to abstain from sexual intercourse, one's innermost spirit will not develop, since the interchange of yin and yang will come to a halt. How could one thus supplement one's vital essence? Blending the vital essence during frequent sexual intercourse, substituting the new energies for the old, is the way to derive real benefit. If a man knows how to make love without emitting semen, then his vital essence will return within. This is the secret of life, which greatly benefits the system.
— Su-Nu-Ching

This is actually a much broader subject in Tantra. The teachings of tantric sexuality tell us that a man can learn to separate the ejaculation from the orgasm and, as a result, experience stronger and longer orgasms – in fact, multiple orgasms are available to the patient, skillful tantric man. It is worth noting here that, biologically speaking, the ejaculatory and orgasmic functions in a man's structure are not the same. The connection between the two is the result of a Pavlovian response, a reflex created in men from a young age that arises when an orgasmic sensation results from sexual stimulation and the ejaculatory mechanism is triggered. But it doesn't have to be the case. In fact Tantra teaches that these two need to be controlled individually. It is not a supernormal feat but rather a matter of education, practice, and consistent effort. And in the case of women, Tantra teaches us that women can experience various forms of orgasm and, most importantly, that women should learn to have implosive, internal orgasms rather than explosive, external ones. Tantra teaches the way to achieve these orgasms and specific techniques exist for both men and women to obtain these skills and integrate them harmoniously into their sexuality.

Let us first focus on the system of the chakras, a subject which has often been represented in a confusing way or misunderstood. The chakras are part of a complex system of energetic centers in the body, through which we can interact with our environment and the universe and can absorb energy. Most ancient traditions recognize chakras, including Chinese medicine, Ayurveda, and *bön* (the original Tibetan religion).

🌸 The first time I felt energies was at a concert listening to pleasant music. Then I had no idea it was energy. At a Tantra course I learned that energies can be induced and directed in myself and others. ... When practicing Tantra I feel energies in chakras and flowing up. I feel a kind of sweet arousing tickle that moves inside my body or concentrates on a point. Sometimes it makes the whole body shiver, it makes me cry or laugh. I feel these sweet vibrations also in chakras, moving eventually all over the body. I have felt this most strongly during sex in the lower abdomen – *manipura* – and in the heart after a backbend. The feeling in the third eye is most strange – a burning feeling. I've also felt the movement of sexual energy in my body. For example, if I hold my hand on the belly of my partner during sex, the hand feels as good as the *lingam*. As if some sweet energy moves via the hand inside the belly. And when pausing, the energy will flow back into me from my partner. It's very pleasing to create an energy circle during hugging. Then it will increase and enlarge... until the whole room is filled with it. I've also felt the sublimation of energies.
— *Martin*

There are seven classic chakras which correspond to the seven levels of the universe – or the seven levels of consciousness:

1) The root chakra, **muladhara**, is located at the midpoint between the anus and testicles for a man or at the entrance of the vagina in a woman.

2) The sacral chakra, **svadhisthana**, is located just above the base of the *lingam* (penis) or area of the clitoris.

3) The solar plexus chakra, **manipura**, is found just below the bellybutton (navel).

4) The heart chakra, **anahata**, is located in the center of the chest in the area of the heart.

5) The throat chakra, **vishuddha**, is found at the base of the pit of the throat.

6) The third eye chakra, **ajna**, is located in the middle of the forehead.

7) The crown chakra, **sahasrara**, located above the top of the head, is considered to be the chakra of pure consciousness. When the female *kundalini* Shakti energy rises to this point, it unites there with the male Shiva energy, and a state of liberating *samadhi* is attained.

All the chakras are located a slight distance outside the body, not inside. Focusing on the chakra correctly is the secret of success in *Hatha Yoga*. During *Hatha Yoga*, as part of a practice of Tantra, one learns various bodily positions or asanas. If we put our bodies into asanas while focusing the mind, energy begins moving, the chakras become activated, and tantric practice starts yielding results. Many Yoga techniques can be done as part of tantric training.

The tantric worldview is a surprisingly complete system which offers very concrete answers and solutions to problems. It provides something that we don't hear at school and home because we lack such traditions and lore and the so-called life-school gives us a very inadequate education.

I am a scientist and engineer by profession and I've been taught to analyze unknown phenomena using the so-called black box method where only the inputs and outputs of a system are observable and what remains unseen must be systemically elaborated and reconstructed. Before coming across Tantra I thought quite negatively about everything esoteric, although I had curiosity. But now I have experienced phenomena that have changed my former worldview.

Understanding the chakra system, their role, and the conscious movement of energy in my body has helped me definitely, for example, to achieve my goals at negotiations and meetings. Also I can change my mood and eliminate fatigue or, on the contrary, I can fall asleep at will.

Meditation skills have helped me achieve my goals. Tantra allows me to live my life more fully.
— *Madis*

A daily practice of *Hatha Yoga* techniques such as *bhadrasana, yoniasana, nasasparshanasana, sarvangasana,* and *shirshasana* is instrumental and supportive to growth in Tantra, making sure the energy flows and a process of sublimation is achieved.

WITHOUT SUBLIMATION THERE IS NO TANTRA

Sublimation is a process in which the vital sexual energies of the human being, which reside at the level of the first three chakras (in particular, the first two), are channeled upward through the body, along the spine and through the body's energetic circuits. This way the sexual energy comes under our control and a man or woman can easily achieve multiple orgasms and especially tantric orgasms.

> The movement of energy during sublimation reminds me a bit of cold shivers, but I'm not cold. It's also like being electrified and sometimes I feel a heat wave. I have gained full control over my sexual energy, withholding ejaculation for as long as I like. It has also brought me to energetic orgasms. At some moment, for instance, the legs or arms become sensitive and there's a feeling that orgasm is also happening in these body parts. Sometimes there are muscle shivers all over my body.
>
> Sometimes I see colors and feel vibrations in different parts of my body while doing *asanas* or *pranayama*.
> — *Madis*

Energy work can be done on two levels. The first level involves learning to feel, sense, and recognize our own pranic energy. *Prana* describes the life force of the human being, also known in the traditions of China and Japan as *chi* or *ki*, respectively. In the Western tradition it is called biomagnetic energy. In the first stage of mastering our energy, we learn how to amplify, control, and channel *prana* through the chakras and throughout the body. This can be done safely even by beginners as long as the teachings are correct.

The second level of energy work involves training with *kundalini* Shakti, which is a much more powerful force.

This energy, once awakened, brings strong symptoms of purification to the human being, which can be challenging if the practitioner is not ready. *Kundalini* is not taught to beginners and it is certainly not recommended to study it from books. I teach it to students who are ready for a *kundalini* program. *Kundalini Yoga* can be taught only after a student has practiced *Hatha Yoga* and *Kriya Yoga* purification techniques, *pranayama*, and meditation for a couple of years minimally under the supervision of a qualified, accomplished teacher. Additionally, in order to begin a *kundalini* training program, such a student must reach a certain level of development, purity, and spiritual maturity, and receive the approval of his or her teacher to start.

❦ Energy during sublimation is like a large tube of energy going directly upward! And inside the tube a huge wave, a flow that takes everything with it. — *Amandine*

HOW TO PREPARE THE BODY, ENERGY, AND MIND

When contemplating the beginnings of tantric practice, the first thing a person should do is to learn how to bring his or her system into a state of high-quality energy. Most people today have many impurities in their systems traceable to poor lifestyle choices related to exercise, diet, stress, and environmental factors. Start by learning to purify yourself and preparing your channels for energy work.

We recommend a healthy diet. Avoid junk food, processed and refined food, and sugar, reduce toxic meat and meat products in general, and avoid bad habits such as smoking, alcohol, drugs, and excessive use of medications. When we adopt a more pure lifestyle, gradually the energy in the body refines into a higher quality.

Put the palms of your hands together and rub them vigorously until you feel your hands energized and that some heat has been created between them. Now stop rubbing and simply hold them a distance apart, trying to feel the sensations in the palms of your hands and the energy between them. This is a very modern technique, simple yet effective, which is even used in the New Age movement. As you do it more often, you can extend your hands further apart while still feeling the energy and can create "energy balls."

A second exercise is for practice with a partner, best done in the nude so that clothes do not obscure any sensations. Put your hands against the hands of your partner. Try to perceive the distinction between your own energy and the energy of your partner, how they are different. Next, sense the energy as you run your hands along your own body, at a slight distance from the skin, and then do the same with your partner on a bed or Yoga mat. Pay attention to the myriad sensations which can arise: differences in temperature, heat or cold, tingling sensations, etc. In some areas the perceiver can literally receive a kinesthetic, direct feeling of blockage – an area which does not emit warm, radiant energy, but rather is dark, cold, unresponsive, and feels naturally stagnant and blocked. Usually when energy flows harmoniously, sensations are warmer and more pleasant and when an area of the body is blocked, the sensations can become colder, unpleasant, and rigid or knotty. Pay attention to your own sensations because, if your intuition tells you there is abnormal or unusual energy, then there is probably some type of blockage there. Usually while you hover above such areas or touch them, there is an intuition to remain there longer. This by itself can create a very nice energetic balance between partners, especially as a prelude to a lovemaking session.

TANTRA IS MEANT FOR THOSE WHO ARE MATURE AND COMMITTED

Tantra has its dangers. Dealing with sexual energy is a little bit like playing with the secrets of the atom. It has enormous potential and it can save humanity, but if used wrongly or amateurishly it can also blow up in our faces. We are talking about very powerful energies – not only the renowned *kundalini* force but also more "magical" energies created with determined tantric intention. Becoming involved without proper knowledge or guidance or approaching it carelessly with improvisation can lead to many complications, some predictable and some unpredictable. Today many teachers claiming to teach Tantra, in workshops or privately, are like children playing with matches. They do not have an awareness of the dangers present and the care required in practice.

❦ I first started feeling energies when I discovered Agama Yoga. My first experience was during the Practical Tantra Workshop with Moses Maimon. I had a tremendous experience. All throughout the workshop, I could feel my forehead quite strongly (knocking and aching sensations) and my arms and hands (burning and stiff). At one point, during a transfiguration meditation, I was not in control at all – it was my first step with Yoga and Tantra. It was like some lightning/thunder of energy came through all of my body and I could not bend my arms or hands – I was paralyzed. I needed to cry, I trembled. I could feel strongly warm/hot hands and energy flowing from my hands through those of my partner for the exercise. Afterwards, I needed an eternity to be able to move (and bend my arms and hands), talk, and breathe!

This workshop was my first step into the Tantra school. At that time I had such amazing feelings and experiences and I'd seen people having such big reactions (for example, orgasms of a man, just in a simple exercise) that I thought something like, "Damn, is it really possible? This man is orgasming right now, and he is not naked and not having concrete sex! Could I one day feel it also? What is this Tantra background? It seems like a parallel universe!! Why has nobody ever taught us that? What is the truth!?"

Now I have more control over energy [and] can direct it.... All of the process is more balanced.

— *Amandine*

Predictable obstacles may be: developing sexual obsessions and fetishes, hurting a partner or losing respect for a partner, falling into the trap of the ego, etc. The wrong guidance or a lack of correct guidance can manifest physically in some imbalances in the body which can even lead to health problems.

Therefore, Tantra offers great promise to any relationship. It can be a great healer and provide a safe, well proven process for a relationship. It provides a framework for true love, the real kind, which can take us to the highest degrees of spirituality. At the same time there are pitfalls, as tantrics warn, so always find a teacher who is authentic and knowledgeable.

Your task is not to seek for love, but merely to seek and find all the barriers within yourself that you have built against it.
— Rumi

IV

TANTRIC SEX

Sexual union is an auspicious Yoga which,
though involving enjoyment of all the sensual
pleasures, gives release. It is a Path to Liberation.
— *Kaularahasya*

CONSCIOUS LOVEMAKING AND THE PROBLEMS OF UNCONSCIOUS OR REGULAR SEXUALITY

For most people the act of sex is a nearly unconscious act. Everyone knows that people at times do impulsive things as a result of their sexual desires and the strong sexual urge. In fact, a close look at history shows many examples of individ-uals who acted irrationally or obses-sively in the name of sex. It truly is the most basic urge.

When we come together for sex, first the longing to touch, kiss, copulate – expressed almost at an animalistic level as physiological needs – leads to the built-up sexual energy of lovemaking. The act then usually ends with an explosive moment called orgasm and the nearly immediate downfall of that orgasmic energy. The tantrics know that this can be a far more refined shared experience, bringing deeper and better sensations and results reaching much further on multiple levels.

If sexuality is so fundamental, how does it manifest in the human being? Each person subtly perceives the sexual chemistry of every other person, emitted through pheromones, and the continuous impulses to attract a partner of the opposite sex. The sexual potential for every human being is vast; many hidden pleasures and dimen-sions of pleasure exist of which most people remain unaware. Sexual education is woefully lacking and even the knowledge of modern sexology has not necessarily reached the average person. People aspire with a goal-oriented mentality and great impatience to reach orgasm as soon as possible. This can lead to a very self-centered approach to lovemaking in which people become absorbed in either chasing their own pleasure or having missed out on it. If both partners have this attitude, it can result in an unsatisfying sex life.

WHY RACE FOR ORGASM?

The tantrics explored this question: What is so important about the orgasm? The human brain produces different chemical elements during orgasm and reaches altered states of consciousness; certainly this is a powerful energetic experience. At the moment of orgasm, the aforementioned polarities are united, at least to a certain degree, which brings effervescence, ecstatic sensations, and a feeling of wholeness. We can say in a technical way that they reach zero polarity. It is something beyond – void, emptiness – resembling what occurs during an electric short circuit. When the positive and negative terminals of a battery are connected with a low-resistance conductor, like a wire, a high current exists, causing the cell to deliver a large amount of energy in a short time.... Potentially this may result in an explosion.

At the time of deep sleep without dream, the consciousness stays in the region of the heart. At the time of dreaming, the consciousness moves to the neck. When one is not sleeping, it is located mainly in the navel region, and when male and female unite sexually in complete harmony and fulfillment, consciousness rests in the heads of the couple.
— Brahmopanishad

If only you could stop during an orgasm to understand what you are feeling…. But most people are so blown away in that state that they cannot even describe it. The tantrics, on the other hand, meditated on that state and found that in the state of orgasm the human being forgets its ego, forgets its name, and forgets the feeling of being separate – he or she reaches the state of oneness, union. Sometimes we describe our most powerful orgasmic experiences as those during which our own body and our lover's cannot be told apart, which explains why the **orgasmic state is a spiritual state** which, according to Tantra, has value.

When great masters of Tantra reached the state of enlightenment and then resumed a normal waking state, their disciples and students asked what it felt like. Surprisingly, the masters said it felt like having an orgasm within every cell of the body. Tantra says that zero in Sanskrit is *shunyata*, or void, which is the same way in which Buddha described the state of enlightenment. **Orgasm in Tantra means surfing very gently on the edge of enlightenment** and for this reason people are very interested to experience it. It is an opening, a door to something higher. The tantrics understood that sexuality is powerful and can take us into very high spheres of being and experience.

ONCE YOU GO TANTRIC, YOU'LL NEVER GO BACK!

Tantra is often mistaken for exotic sex performed in fancy, complicated positions such as those depicted in the *Kama Sutra*. But, in fact, Tantra has nothing to do with that ancient sensual guide, although it probably represents the strongest association in an average Westerner's mind. The tantric union is more precisely about energetic awareness than sensuality. The first important point is that tantrics understood the sexual interaction to be a dance of plus and minus inside us that creates almost everything in our lives. Any energy according to Tantra has two aspects; this is the basic polarity, which is defined as plus and minus. In Chinese Taoism it is called yin and yang, whereas in psychotherapy it is called animus and anima. We can say that the purpose of Yoga (Yoga means "union") is to unite exactly these two polar aspects into one, thus bringing the desired unity. In *Hatha Yoga*, the words *ha* and *tha* stand for sun and moon, respectively, another example of the union of polarities. These dynamics define our interaction with other human beings, including the relationship between men and women.

While in a mundane view, our passion and sexual desire can be understood as a simple animalistic need for copulation, the tantrics say that sexual attraction is a physical manifestation of a higher type of attraction. They realized that this sexual attraction is actually a tremendous force; by mixing plus and minus we can reach enormous power. During tantric sexual interaction, the partners become very conscious of their sexual energy, their awareness heightens, and they begin to channel energy throughout their bodies, most immediately for the purpose of deepening and prolonging orgasm until reaching high states of consciousness. Later this energy, still greatly amplified, may be directed for the purpose of obtaining better results in nearly any area of life we choose.

❀ Tantra has made me happier with myself and with life. At a tantric massage course I understood what true love is. It has helped me gain contentment with myself and the world.
— *Liina*

During the tantric union, the level of sexual pleasure may become hundreds of times more powerful and satisfying than it is during an average sexual union. Both the man and woman can experience it far more deeply. The orgasms can be much more powerful, satisfying, and long-lasting. The difference between tantric sex and regular sex is so vast that most people who have once tasted tantric practice will never choose to go back. But for that, of course, both partners have to learn. The woman should learn how to surrender into deep orgasm, and the man should learn how to give these orgasms to her. Once those states of pleasure are triggered, both will learn to surf the "valley of orgasm." Entering that state is one thing, but remaining there is another entirely. Indeed, one of the next challenges is learning how to prolong the orgasmic state – for both partners – and to sustain the ability to "surf the orgasmic wave" for longer and longer periods of time.

One should bear in mind that, while a couple may enjoy either short or long-lasting lovemaking sessions, time must not be a factor. It is true that Tantra at its core is a slower type of sexuality, lasting longer, but there are no time limits or demands. Many people who are uninitiated in Tantra wonder, if I practice Tantra and learn to control my sexual energy, how will I know when to stop having sex? Normally, in typical sex there is physical proof – the symphony has concluded and the sign is obvious in the form of ejaculation.

The answer to the question of when to stop is the same whether you practice Tantra or not – you have a clear feeling of satisfaction. There is no need to create any physiological exaggeration; rather you make love until, despite that passion remains, it simply feels like a good time to stop. This is determined individually, couple to couple, based on energetic factors as well as psychological and emotional feedback.

One can learn to prolong an orgasm, but to rest there in that state consciously is difficult. For most people it is a very short experience, about 15 seconds. It can feel like standing in a deserted train station, watching the train approach suddenly and just as quickly depart in a flash. The experience has been too short to be understood – it is quite hard to understand and be conscious about what you feel in mere seconds. By increasing the length and intensity of that experience, we open the window of opportunity that leads to greater and greater self-awareness. The tantric tradition provides the earnest practitioner with guidance every step of the way.

Some people might wonder whether tantric sexuality takes the spontaneous fun out of sex with its breathing exercises, muscle squeezing, and *Hatha Yoga* techniques. But learning tantric sex is like learning any skill in life. When you learn how to drive a car, it is also a very mechanical and maybe not so relaxed experience in the beginning. Five years later while driving a car, you may be simultaneously talking on your mobile phone and may not even remember exactly how to drive – it has become so automatic. The same is true with Tantra; the more you practice, the more it becomes second nature, requiring less of your conscious attention.

Tantra doesn't remove any spontaneity from lovemaking. Different people need different levels of training. Some are naturally gifted, finding results in just weeks, while others less gifted or harboring blockages may require several months or more to reach success in Tantra. Never worry about how long it will take to train. Even if it takes one year, in the whole scale of life, wouldn't that be worth it in order to reach a much higher-quality level of sexuality for the 50 years that are still to come? Tantra can change your relationships, the way you feel about your body, and so many more aspects of life. For those who are willing to take the first step, Tantra will take 20 steps toward them.

TANTRA IS A POWERFUL PATH OF TRANSFORMATION

As a conscious path of sexuality, it is most often the case that Tantra will require some training in the beginning. However, once mastered it can completely transform your sexual life. At the beginner's level, a woman needs to learn how to be conscious during orgasm, and then the actual practice of controlling the sexual energy begins, revealing Shakti in her glory, the exquisite femininity of each woman.

What is femininity? Is it the essence of a woman who appears very sexy to observers? Or is it something deeper? In Tantra women learn what real femininity is. If a man and woman develop these aspects in tandem, when they make love in a tantric manner, the connection is many times more powerful, intense, and satisfying.

❧ Tantric principles – like the concept of woman as a goddess – have clearly helped me to see through the superficial and very limited understanding of femininity prevalent in society, based on the assessment of all kinds of external aspects. Through Tantra I have started to believe in my own divinity. I don't compare myself with other women. On the contrary, whereas previously I perceived competitors, instead I now also see their unique divinity – it is a very liberating experience that makes me happy. By practicing tantric femininity I have become gentler, more caring and warm, and at the same time playful and much more free. Instead of the former good girl, there is an internally free woman who enjoys herself and others, being spontaneous and sometimes naughty. My husband says that I now have a sensual look – a look that seems to undress – and he enjoys it greatly.

— *Tiina*

Men starting out in Tantra need to learn how to retain their *ojas*, the life force bound up with the sexual energy, Shakti. If a man loses the *ojas* and there is no *brahmacharya*, then unfortunately there is no Tantra. The next steps are to control the sexual energy and learn how to circulate it throughout the body, for which there are various techniques. The phase which then follows brings deeper states of awareness and energy. This is a state which is hard to describe and should be experienced.

Tantric sexuality also brings results of another kind. A man practicing Tantra may develop, whether or not he notices, various aspects of masculinity as a result of the sublime tantric energies. Tantra reveals to a man the nature of true masculinity, which is far from being macho or overly sensitive. Both show a crisis of identity in extremes – a man not really knowing what he is supposed to do as a man.

For both genders to achieve these results, it is necessary to dedicate ourselves, creating the time to practice, and making an effort. It requires commitment, regular practice, and training, and not everybody is ready for this. To know the secrets of Tantra is a great gift, like wielding a magic wand. However, a certain karma will be in effect in each person's destiny with Tantra. Some will be built for Tantra and it will come naturally for them; these ones will dedicate themselves without turning back. Others, under the influence of destiny and conditions in our current *yuga*, or cycle of time, will find greater challenges in Tantra. From an observer's point of view, choosing a destiny that involves Tantra may appear like a test for them. They may be made for Tantra, but will they hear about it? They may hear about it and even learn about it, but will they practice it? They may practice it, but without the diligence for results, and so on. As mentioned, our current *yuga* presents a greater challenge for all of us.

All spiritual practices in this era take more effort. Tantra is no different, and a commitment will be necessary to realize the transformation which is possible.

❀ I was attracted to Tantra by the possibility of integrating sexual life with spiritual evolution. I always loved sex but considered it like something a bit forbidden without knowing why. Also the idea of integrating all life events into spirituality attracted me to tantric spirituality. There is no need to leave and go to a cave. I can practice spirituality in the world and not be apart from it. Before Tantra, life was having a job, money, etc., and one day, death. The end. Now life is an adventure, trying to discover who I am. The understanding of the structure of the human being, experiencing different emotions, mind, consciousness, and what will make me truly happy and what won't helps a lot. I now try to get answers from the soul and not from the outside world. I love the system of Tantra; I know it's a true path, a true practice of evolution.

— Joss

V

THE TANTRIC WOMAN

Throughout history, women have been the embodiment of beauty, grace, and sensuality, captured poetically by thousands if not millions of writers, given shape by the artists and sculptors of time, and immortalized through song since the minstrels of yore.... Unfortunately for most women in modern times, their sensuality is not very well developed; the demands of family and career life seem to simply intercede, preventing its full expression. In Tantra women learn how to become more sensual and to form a better connection with their own sexuality. Even if a woman does express her sensual nature, by enhancing this quality more and more, she can access higher levels of ecstasy. As woman is the source of power in Tantra, the Shakti in the relationship, her body has the capacity for resonance with an ultimate level of femininity. The more sensual she becomes, the more pleasure a couple can experience because the man is like a mirror to the woman's pleasure. When a woman becomes more feminine and sensual, and the man becomes masculine and emissive, their polarity is amplified, and both are brought to higher levels of pleasure and even deeper orgasms.

The majority of women nowadays have a lot of sexual blockages and Tantra can help remove these efficiently. While women need more time to open up and arouse their sexual desire and sexual energy, they can learn not only how to experience orgasm but how to have different types of orgasm. The truth is that all women can orgasm, and according to Tantra, all women *can* experience a broad range of orgasms.

❀ I have felt the movement of sexual energy in my body, the energy moving as a hot stripe from the lower body that spreads all over my body. Orgasms don't have to be only sexual. I like the *karezza* techniques where waves of energy are moved without touching the body. The heart activates very strongly, energy is directed up from the lower body (I don't know why this happens), and the orgasmic area is in the energy fields of the upper body. The mind switches off. It's like someone, some higher wisdom, is guiding you. An energetic explosion occurs that heals the body and our lives, and those around you. We are all connected.

— *Ülle*

WOMEN ARE NATURAL-BORN TANTRICS

Women have an intrinsically better resonance with the universe. As Shakti means not only woman but goddess, thus the universe has a feminine quality; Shakti is that energy which creates and manifests this world. As a woman is born in a feminine structure, she is better equipped to live in the world, too. Tantrics say it beautifully: A woman's body is a rare musical instrument. If a man is a skillful musician who can create divine music with his lover, then the potential of a woman's body is magical and goes far beyond just having satisfying sex. A woman's body can produce huge quantities of energy that generate transformation for both herself and her partner, bringing them both to new spiritual heights and even altered consciousness.

How delicious an instrument is woman, when artfully played upon; how capable is she of producing the most exquisite harmonies, of executing the most complicated variations of love, and of giving the most divine of erotic pleasures.
— Ananda Ranga

Tantrics say **women can bring spiritual feelings into manifestation**. Pleasure itself can be generated, especially the woman's pleasure. This is very important in Tantra – how to bring a woman to pleasure. In Tantra – unlike the average daily life that plays out across the planet – it is impossible for a man to have pleasure and a woman not to. That is simply not tantric sex! On the relationship level, this represents an extremely disappointing waste of energy, like taking a Stradivarius violin and using it to hammer nails into a wall. A complete waste! But then again, Tantra is not for everybody; it requires an open mind and deep interest. A person needs not only to have the right karma but also to be shown grace to receive these teachings. Even in the India of ancient times, Tantra wasn't for everyone, despite that the knowledge was quite widely spread even as its spiritual level generally and gradually has been declining for a long time due to various historical reasons.

ON THE MENU TONIGHT: SEVEN TYPES OF ORGASM

For the average modern woman these days, the main issue that comes up worldwide is that not all women experience orgasm. Some researchers say that approximately 70 to 80 percent of women orgasm, but 20 to 30 percent don't experience it at all. And of those who experience orgasm, many experience only one type of orgasm, the clitoral orgasm, which is usually the most limited type. Many claim that they can only reach orgasm by stimulating themselves, whereas others simply cannot experience orgasm during sexual penetration. Often, in frustration, women end up pleasing themselves after their partners collapse following ejaculation. It is worth mentioning here that the differing arousal phases for men and women contribute to the lack of synchronicity in orgasm and even the potential during sexual union. This is in large part due to the lack of proper sexual education, especially for men.

But women have much more potential. By virtue of being born in the body of woman, they have a connection to the principle of Shakti. Women have a very powerful capacity of resonance, like an incredible radio station which has the ability to interact with energies which men sometimes cannot. Many tantric masters say that women are natural-born tantrics under the right circumstances.

My teacher taught me, and I also verified in my own practice, that woman can experience seven different types of orgasm. Clitoral orgasm is the first one at the beginners' level, and it is quite weak, localized, and not very intense. This most closely resembles the male ejaculatory orgasm – quick, sharp, and abrupt. Most women are not left very satisfied. According to Tantra, women can reach much more – mind-blowing orgasms which have incredible effects. Pleasure multiplies and touches them deeply, answering their needs and opening up the heart chakra. In Tantra all women can have this. There is magic waiting for you, ladies!

Problems stem from our modern society and the fact that we live in *Kali Yuga*. Women and men are not taught about sexuality, which is expected to "come naturally." But in Tantra it is very important to teach people about sexuality properly – and not just the basic facts, which are by far not good enough. Sex is such an essential part of our life, it affects everything. Even Dr. Sigmund Freud said that the basic motivation for human beings is sex and yet this is left to chance, especially for women – sensitive and incredible goddesses who often do not fully tap their inherent feminine potential.

IN TANTRA THERE ARE FIVE CLASSIC TYPES
OF ORGASM:

- The first orgasm is called the clitoral orgasm.
- The second is the lower vaginal orgasm,
  usually connected with the opening to the vagina.
- The third is called the inner vaginal orgasm, which in-
  cludes the very important and famous G-spot orgasm.
- The fourth orgasm is called the cervical-uterine
  orgasm,the deepest and most tantric orgasm.
- The fifth type is the anal orgasm.

AND TWO SPECIAL TYPES ROUND OUT
THE SEVEN FORMS OF ORGASM:

- The sixth is an orgasm at the level of the nipples.
- The seventh is called the urinary orgasm.

How to have them all? Tantra is usually taught within the context of a workshop exactly so that participants have the time to understand all the aspects and learn how to achieve them or help their partner reach these states. Nevertheless, I would like to sum up the vital points related to each of these orgasms:

The first orgasm, the clitoral orgasm, originates from the stimulation of an organ in the genitals of a woman, the clitoris. This organ has been hailed in modern sexology as the gateway to real pleasure and as the saving point for a woman who wants to take charge of her own pleasure and gain sexual independence. In Tantra, the stimulation of the clitoris, while an essential part of sexuality, is not the main part of it by far. This orgasm is difficult to control and is thus similar to the male orgasm.

Clitoral stimulation usually brings a localized sensation that can peak at an orgasmic level, albeit an orgasm that is limited, vehement, and not deep. It is true that in rare cases, some women find deeper satisfaction with a clitoral orgasm. But normally those are women who, due to their specific structure, tend to generate two and sometimes three orgasms together with the clitoral orgasm as a kind of "package deal." In most cases, however, the clitoral orgasm is quite limited.

The second type of orgasm, the lower vaginal orgasm, is an orgasm connected to the root chakra of the woman and therefore it also may be heavy and difficult to control (although not as difficult as the clitoral orgasm). It is already deeper and brings more sensual and beneficial sensations. It tends to be more feminine and is usually favored by women with a strong activation of the root chakra.

The third type of orgasm is the inner vaginal orgasm. This one is already much more feminine in nature, therefore deep, more satisfying, and with great potential for considerably more pleasure than the previous two. This orgasm activates the second chakra and is related to the water element, bringing much more pleasure but also many more feelings beyond the physical sensations. This type of orgasm – which often triggers shaking, tremors, crying, screaming, and other emotional manifestations – has a few subcategories, meaning that it may develop into a few types of its own, notably the famous G-spot orgasm.

The G-spot orgasm is already a full-blown tantric orgasm that can bring multiple orgasms in its wake. It touches the woman deeply in her heart and soul and usually involves tremendous satisfaction. It can involve muscular contractions in the vagina and in many cases a certain ejaculation of fluid, usually referred to as the female ejaculation. In Tantra this mysterious fluid is known as *kalas*. Due to the widespread lack of sexual education, women often think that they have urinated when in fact they ejaculated. Chemical analysis has shown that the fluid is not urine, although trace urine may be present. Some sexologists consider that this ejaculated fluid is a mixture of lubricating fluid, a liquid from the paraurethral glands, fluid from the Bartholin's glands, and a small quantity of urine. But since the quantity of this fluid may sometimes reach a half-liter or even full liter, this is not an entirely satisfactory explanation. Therefore, the tantrics believe a special energy materializes as this fluid.

The fourth type of orgasm is the cervical-uterine orgasm, originating from stimulation of a woman's cervix. This is the ultimate of all the tantric orgasms and the one that all tantric women aspire to reach. It brings a multi-orgasmic pleasure without end, shaking the soul, bringing natural states of meditation, ecstasy, and in some cases higher states of consciousness.

The anal orgasm is derived from anal stimulation and anal sex. Tantrics accept the fact that anal sex can be pleasurable and beneficial, if done correctly and with care and love. Not all women are inclined to enjoy such stimulation, which in Tantra is of course understandable and completely acceptable. Since the most important orgasms are the third and, more so, fourth, this one is optional and not mandatory at all. From my experience, about one woman in five is attracted to exploring and discovering this orgasm. The anal orgasm can be very powerful and pleasurable, and is considered a tantric orgasm as well. In some cases it may also relieve some psychological complexes for women who suffer from anal retentive tendencies. In Tantra these may be considered the result of blocked energy in that area, which anal orgasms can help remedy. In addition, for some women with heavy energy stagnating in the root chakra, anal sex and orgasm can help sublimate this energy.

The sixth orgasm is the nipple orgasm. Tantrics consider that the nipples are connected energetically to the clitoris and therefore stimulation of the nipples may produce a strong orgasm on its own. From my experience, when I taught women how to achieve such an orgasm, it seemed first of all that not all women are sensitive enough in the nipples to experience this. However, with consistent sensitizing and re-energizing of the breasts and nipples, even those women who ordinarily don't feel much, will experience beautiful, orgasmic feelings. And those who are already sensitive, this can even lead to mind-blowing experiences.

The urinary orgasm is a very unique and peculiar type of orgasm. Indeed, it involves a tantric aptitude and inclination, but more importantly it relies on an open mind. In Tantra (and later in modern sexology) it was discovered that when a woman's G-spot is stimulated, often she reports feeling the need to urinate. Women who have an open mind and are relaxed enough to actually allow themselves to urinate while being stimulated in this way are many times surprised to find out that they enter a very special orgasmic state. Therefore, in Tantra this has been developed into an independent orgasm called the urinary orgasm. For this tantric women may purposefully drink water before the sexual union and bring themselves to the edge of orgasm (with their tantric partner) before urinating as orgasm begins. The result is a strong amplification of the orgasmic pleasure to such a degree that it becomes a powerful orgasmic experience known as the urinary orgasm.

There is much more information in Tantra regarding these orgasms and how to realize each of them. Unfortunately, this is the kind of tantric information and teaching that must be given directly by a teacher, in workshops and with proper explanation, or in relationships in which one partner has mastered a tantric practice (but still, theoretical background would be necessary for fully understanding it). But hopefully this summary allows the reader to get a glimpse into the tantric approach to the topic of female orgasm.

❦ I have experienced various female orgasms. During G-spot orgasms I have felt strong arousal, peeing sensations, energy moving up in my body and into my head. More electrical sensations and clarity. I remember once or twice some *kalas* came out during lovemaking. Then I felt a release of pressure, and tiredness....

Anal orgasms have been so strong and pleasurable. I can feel a huge amount of energy in my spine and a buzz in the head and whole body. Cervical orgasms make me feel like I'm drunk and spaced out. It's a diffused sensation all over the place. More cloudy. During clitoral orgasms I feel strong arousal, without explosion as the pleasure starts from the clitoris and goes into the vagina and deeper.

Sexually, I never had so much pleasure before Tantra.

— *Amandine*

WHAT ABOUT ANAL SEX?

Tantra accepts any form of pleasure which is reached with respect and love for one's partner, and thus tantric sexuality includes anal sex as well. In Tantra anal orgasm, one of the seven types of orgasm, can be very satisfying and is especially helpful for women with a lot of vitality or very heavy energy because it will easily sublimate this energy. Anal sex can be a very deep experience which activates the higher chakras. While it is considered beautiful, of course it requires making an extra effort with cleanliness; both partners should specially wash themselves before and after anal sex.

Many tantrics enjoy anal sex regularly, but know that it demands a different approach than regular lovemaking. To enjoy anal lovemaking, a woman needs to be very relaxed and feel eminently cared for in order to surrender herself fully and open herself to the experience. Massaging the area beforehand can be a helpful precursor in order to relax and diminish any tension, the primary factor that may inhibit full enjoyment. A man, on the other hand, must develop himself as a lover so he knows how to have anal sex properly (which is not as shown in porn movies!). You don't just penetrate the woman and move with full power. Anal sex needs to be approached very gently and slowly, with consideration and care for the partner, with good communication and listening skills, and an intuitive feeling for the partner's body and energy. Also a tantric man can learn the rare skill of controlling the strength of his erection, so he can choose whether to exhibit a very strong or softer erection, allowing him to tune into his partner more deeply.

When engaging in anal sex with a woman, it is helpful for a man to start out with a somewhat soft erection or semi-erection and enter her gently and slowly. (In Tantra, learning to increase or reduce the erection on command is learned as part of men's practices.) In another method, the man does not move at all, and it is the woman who moves her buttocks to determine the pace and depth of penetration. The anal structure includes two sphincter muscles at its entrance. Once the penis pushes past those muscles, anal sex becomes much easier, discomfort eases considerably or disappears altogether, and anal sex usually becomes more pleasurable. Even women who absolutely love anal sex most often want to proceed slowly in the beginning each time, until these sphincters have relaxed. Sex of any kind does not have to include the act of pumping or sliding back and forth; remember that it can also be enjoyed in complete stillness or with very little movement. Following full penetration, regular or anal, a couple can just remain in union, using very small movements or none, concentrating on the flow of energy. Extremely powerful orgasms can come from this style of lovemaking.

OVERCOMING FEAR IS A FEAT WORTH ACHIEVING

In modern times tantrics have observed that many women tend to develop sexual blockages, some of which are complex and held in the cellular memory of their beings. Generally speaking, one of women's main problems is their lack of orgasm. Some women have to literally race for their orgasm – because they know men usually don't last for very long, so they reason that they need to also reach some orgasm quickly before their partner is finished. Modern statistics say that in a good (and average) scenario, a man can last from five to 10 minutes before he ejaculates and is spent. This is also mentioned in the Kinsey Reports from the 1950s; see the books of Dr. Alfred Kinsey *et al: Sexual Behavior in the Human Male* (1948) and *Sexual Behavior in the Human Female* (1953).

Women are different – they need to open up slowly, to enter those deep stages, to enjoy lovemaking. It takes a while. Women don't have an on/off switch. People in today's modern era lack information; all they know about sex is learned through masturbation or porn, which both represent very poor ways to learn about lovemaking and sexuality. Porn and masturbation tend to be very mechanical and most likely no real knowledge about sexual skills or arts is transmitted. So men will be very clumsy and women will develop many blockages. Women tend to carry personal traumas or complex, unprocessed emotions in their genital area and organs. The vagina is a reflexive organ, like the feet and eyes, which holds negative experiences and partially "closes" as a result (not necessarily physically, although the condition of vagismus involves a subconscious physical blocking of this area). It is more that parts of its receptivity and expression are shut down, blocking its ability to be responsive and open. Personal and psychological blockages can be infinite in number and create problems for a woman's health and relationships. It is relatively easy to overcome them in Tantra if men and women are willing to make an effort.

Many women feel that they are not empowered to make love and express their femininity, as if it makes them appear cheap or too sexually obsessed. They may not even know they have that potential and, without a demonstration, they think that sex is just a big disappointment so they block themselves psychologically. Other women have never experienced pleasure with sex, so it is more like an exercise to keep their partner happy. The race for orgasm, which takes place when a woman thinks she has to reach orgasm quickly because her partner doesn't last long, can leave a woman alone if she loses and eventually must take care of her own pleasure with a dildo and masturbation.

Sexual problems can manifest as pain in the body. Psychological blockages lead to psychosomatic pain in the *yoni*, the yogic name for vagina, which can lead to the manifestation of various conditions and diseases. Tantra takes all that and resolves it. But the resolution is not necessarily simple, because frequently women, especially in Western countries, come to Tantra long after they have begun their sexual lives and they are already quite scarred. Consequently, the psychological patterns and traumas are often already huge and very well programmed. Then we are talking not about learning something new, but first about recovering and healing the old issues.

In such cases, we must first put our attention on healing and only then can we talk about advanced tantric practices.

How do we do it? There are various ways. Tantric massage is great for this. When men don't know how to make love properly, at least in the beginning they can learn how to do tantric massage, which is not difficult. In so doing, the problem of control isn't confronted, because there is no sex yet. By practicing certain techniques women can start slowly relieving pressures and blockages. Some women may cry during these sessions, which is very good. While challenging, it is important to keep moving forward to make progress on this path, with or without a partner.

Some women claim that because they don't have a partner, they can't practice Tantra. This is not true at all. Any woman can still practice many techniques on her own, and when she finds a partner she won't be starting from zero. As a woman, you can build up your stamina, learn to feel your own energies, and learn how to have multiple orgasms by yourself. You'll start to feel and know your body better, to become more skillful. When you are an experienced lover you'll also find a suitable partner much more easily. So Tantra is also very useful for singles.

Here in this body are the sacred rivers; here are the sun and moon, as well as all the pilgrimage places. I have not encountered another temple as blissful as my own body.
— Saraha Doha

EXERCISE: SELF-STIMULATING
TANTRIC MASSAGE FOR WOMEN

Find a free hour or two for practice when you will not be disturbed. Turn off your mobile device and lock the door to your room. Feel free to light some candles or incense. It may also be nice to take a shower as part of setting the mood. Most of all, make sure you feel comfortable.

Lie down on your bed and relax. Take a few deep breaths in and out, feeling yourself relax more deeply with each exhalation. Allow yourself to let go of everything that demanded your attention on this day.

Remove all your clothes (but be sure you are warm and comfortable) and begin by caressing your body, breasts, thighs, abdomen, and face. Be gentle with yourself and don't rush; just take your time. When you start feeling more pleasure and attunement with your body, make your way to your *yoni* (vagina). Caress and gently run the first and second fingers of your right hand (or left, if you are left-handed) over the outer lips of your *yoni*. Feel the pleasure and keep your mind present and focused on your moment-to-moment sensations.

At some point you will notice that the inner lips of your *yoni* seem to be opening up and "inviting" you in. At this point, insert one or two fingers and start gently touching inside the first few centimeters past the entrance of your *yoni*.

Apply very mild pressure and explore your *yoni*'s entrance, being aware of the enhanced sensations you feel. At this point try to notice a lumpy, slightly raised area on the upper wall of your *yoni*, perhaps about four to six centimeters from the entrance. This is your G-spot, which will become more pronounced the more sexually aroused you are. Slighty massage it and become more and more aware of the sensations you're feeling. When you feel ready, slowly come to a stop, and relax. (The next steps of this massage will be taught at a later stage.)

VI

TANTRA FOR MEN

Tantric men learn to control their own sexual energy and become much more aware of their ejaculatory functions and how they experience pleasure. Men should learn to defocus the pleasure on the genitals, and to spread it throughout the body and into the higher chakras.

Men have different approaches to sex, as they tend to learn it within a context of performance. Since they tend to be competitive by nature, men often compare sex with sports, which is a totally useless way of looking at sex. A man should view his sexuality in terms of **becoming a master of love**. Sex is not something to "get over with" quickly, and men should be willing to understand how to approach it in a different way, unlearning bad habits and cultivating a new era in their masculine life.

❦ My biggest discovery in Tantra has been the existence of powerful energies and the possibility of controlling them. Also the unforgettable pleasure experienced in tantric sex, when the woman pulls the man with her when approaching orgasm. Thus far the best experience has been a very strong and fast flow of energy when the woman is approaching orgasm, as a result of which I felt amazing pleasure and sparkling in my whole body. My tantric sexual experiences have been so powerful that it would be hard to return to usual practice. I'm certainly a much better lover thanks to Tantra – I feel more concentrated and masculine. In this sense, Tantra has changed my life.
— *Allan*

Men mostly think of sex as a ride to ejaculation accompanied by an explosive orgasm. For many men, unfortunately, that is the top of the top. Masturbation teaches them how to quickly achieve some form of satisfaction, which is usually followed by a weakened, depleted feeling because the energy has declined. For a man this may be described as a feeling of relaxation. If the pressure builds up again, a man may start to feel horny again and want to relieve the pressure. That seems to often be the only factor – the pressure is annoying and a man wants to release it. As a result, a man may at times get into a bad mood and become agitated, maybe even to the point of starting an argument with his partner if she is not helping him release this pressure and he feels he can't work and function normally. It is as if sex is an enemy and he needs to conquer it.

From Tantra's point of view, this approach lacks a vital understanding of the immense importance of the *ojas* Shakti, which is lost. Men don't realize the great gift they have. The pressure is not some annoying thing that you need to get rid of in any way possible. On the contrary, men; **it is the secret of your power**. Instead of fighting it and approaching it from a competitive standpoint, **learn how to control it. This is the true measure of a man, at least from a sexual standpoint**.

For many men this approach sounds annoying and like too much work. It is much easier to have a beer and pizza, watch football, get quick sexual relief, and then life is OK. Such men sail through life conveniently and don't want to make any efforts whatsoever. They don't understand that by doing so they are missing out on their own power.

*Breath, thought, and semen are the three constituents
of the Enlightenment Potential. They should be harmonized
and consciously controlled. The yogi who brings together
breath, thought, and semen becomes the Indestructible One,
endowed with transcendental spontaneity.*
— Kalachakra Tantra

STEP INTO YOUR TRUE POWER

When a man decides to consciously and truly enhance his masculinity and fulfill his own nature, controlling his own energies, this is the true measure of heroism and masculinity, summarized in the tantric concept of *Vira*. If a man feels pressure in his lower body, he doesn't need to "get over it." If he learns how to perceive it, control it, and channel it, he becomes a hero in the real sense. Ancient heroes were heroes at this level as well. To become a sexually powerful lover who can give women the deepest orgasmic experiences of their lives, true tenderness, and full satisfaction, a man needs first of all to identify himself properly, to agree deeply with his true nature – which is what is meant by "conquering oneself." This is the first lesson in becoming a tantric man.

That kind of achievement has a huge impact on everything else men do in life, beginning with relationships but extending to the work and business front. Men say they want power. Well, this is the real power. Men attribute their aggressive, violent natures to sexual dissatisfaction or frustration. This is simply not the case; the problem is that they let their own sexuality loose instead of controlling it. This is the difference gained by men who treat their lovers with respect, displaying the patience to remain centered and focused, with the ability to go deep – which shows that you control your own nature. Tantra doesn't solve all the problems in the world, but it does teach us to be more peaceful, loving people leading meaningful lives.

Of practical changes, I consider the most important to be that – thanks to Tantra – I am a more masculine man. My confidence, will, and ability to concentrate are stronger than before Tantra, and I can also deal better with negative emotions thanks to tantric techniques and self-observation. I see the world surrounding me as much more diverse and colorful than before, offering possibilities for solutions and development in every moment. Previously, my ego would feel affected and make me react in defense each time I felt someone criticized me. Today my ego has become much more tolerant toward everything and sees more positive (a possibility) in everything than negative. I have many fewer defensive blockages than before starting Tantra….

Not long ago, external factors like the moods of a woman, jealousy, problems with work and partners, and other life situations – often quite insignificant things – could influence my feelings greatly, pushing me out of balance and thereby breaking my confidence. It was easy to insult or enrage me. I often felt like I was being hurt. I was like a capricious child in a sense. Today I can say that I stand on a much firmer ground. I try to recognize the arising emotions quickly and don't allow them to rage. Many of the situations that used to make me emotional are not problematic any more. I have started to realize the meaning of possibilities. A situation can be both negative and positive, depending on the attitude. Before, situations had only one meaning or interpretation – my interpretation. The understanding of the multitude of possibilities and viewpoints and the desire to take them into account has helped me keep my relationships better and solve problems better. I have managed to avoid many problems by conscious attitude.

Surely, tantric practices have helped me achieve greater confidence and balance. Also they have helped me feel feelings that I had no idea these existed before, like real happiness and love.

— *Allan*

The fact is when we control our ejaculation we do not lose pleasure. Many men fear that when ejaculation is taken away, the last pleasure in their lives will be removed. But actually nothing is taken away, **because ejaculation and orgasm biologically are not the same thing. Orgasm and ejaculation function through different neurological mechanisms. With training we can learn to enhance orgasm, extend it, and multiply it to amazing dimensions. But first we need to learn how to control the physical act of ejaculation. After that men can experience pleasure which is far superior and truly incredible.** I have taught men to achieve this control; in the beginning they couldn't believe it was possible and were dubious. And then they started to have orgasms without erections or ejaculations. So while it will take some work to undo this physiological association, orgasm and ejaculation aren't necessarily connected – no matter what you've been told – and it is incredibly beautiful what can be achieved when we learn this control.

❧ I have experienced orgasms without ejaculation and full-body orgasms during energetic massage when shivers go through the body. The length of sexual intercourse has prolonged considerably. I have developed the ability to withdraw ejaculation, keep the energy, raise it, and channel it into my head to use for spiritual activities. However, it seems as if it is like an honor thing for women to squeeze energy from men. ☺ When intercourse ends without ejaculation they are astonished or confused at first: "What do you mean – don't you like me?" This speaks to the misconception in society that pleasure is not understood correctly.
— *Martin*

Many men worry about so-called "blue balls," a slang term indicating tension, congestion, aching, or even pain in the groin area experienced by some but not all men following states of arousal that don't end with ejaculation. They think that if they don't have sex for a few days the testicles will become painful or even swollen. The body produces sperm continually and traditional Western doctors always advise men that it is important to ejaculate regularly or they may suffer consequences to their health. The doctor is right from one standpoint: If you don't know what to do with the sexual energy and merely let it accumulate and stagnate at the level of the second chakra, then it can cause problems and imbalances.

However, Tantra relies on a different approach, which can be called transmutation. According to the ancient dictums of Tantra, if a man channels his sexual energy upward and circulates it in the body, doing tantric practice daily or at least four to five times per week in addition to *Hatha Yoga* techniques for balancing and sublimation, then he will open up some of his channels, especially certain lymph channels which are not active in most people. At this point the sperm will begin to be reabsorbed into the body. Once that happens, in a process that takes a few weeks or even months, those specific lymph channels will begin to open, the sperm will be reabsorbed into the body and circulated to the higher chakras, and this will bring a huge level of rejuvenation. Modern medicine does not confirm or accept this, but tantrics have known it to be the actual result of tantric practice for centuries.

It's also very important that a man's lifestyle be as pure as possible, which means avoiding alcohol, smoking, and junk food, minimizing meat in the diet and the use of antibiotics and medications, and reducing stress. All of these things contribute impurities to the body, which impede the proper movement of energy. We would say that it's one thing to make small excesses occasionally, another to live in a state of excess. It can be very beneficial to purify through a detox program or *Kriya Yoga* (as described in the *Hatha Yoga Pradipika* – the teaching of the six acts of purification) and thus to eliminate these negative factors from the system. Some men resist giving up all these so-called pleasures in life, and subsequently they also encounter obstacles in following the tantric path. However, when you purify your body in this way, and learn to transmute your energy you will encounter no problems with "blue balls."

EXERCISE: SELF-STIMULATING
TANTRIC MASSAGE FOR MEN

Find a free hour or two for practice when you will not be disturbed. Turn off your mobile device and lock the door to your room. Feel free to light some candles or incense. It may also be nice to take a shower as part of setting the mood. Most of all, make sure you feel comfortable.

Lie down on your bed and relax. Take a few deep breaths in and out, feeling yourself relax more deeply with each exhalation. Allow yourself to let go of everything that demanded your attention on this day. You may also wish to practice in a sitting position if this is more comfortable.

Start by gently caressing your chest, abdomen, thighs, and face, making your way down to your genitalia and testicles. Touch your *lingam* (penis) softly, noticing the sensations of pleasure you feel.

As you proceed, a semi-erection will begin to emerge. Make sure you do not allow yourself to become too excited. Simply allow yourself, with slow caresses and your complete focus on the sensations you are able to perceive, to feel vibrations in this area and to become more and more attuned to those sensations. Stop here and slowly calm down until you are able to conclude your session. (The next steps to this technique will be taught later on.)

VII

MODERN SEXUALITY

Early tantrics pondered how they could improve their sexuality, as it was such a basic impulse impacting all aspects of life. And then they asked what would happen if they could study this orgasmic state further and find out how to extend it – how to make it deeper, comprehensive, more powerful – and they discovered how. In the same way, in modern times people also contemplate how they can improve their sex lives.

When a people are sexually frustrated and chronically unsatisfied, it affects how they feel, how they relate to others, and how they perform at work. People are offended by that sometimes – especially those who are more educated, rational, or socially well positioned. They say to themselves: "I can control my sexual urges – I am not an animal. Rather, I'm a very serious and sophisticated person." But even these people should remember Freud's explanation that all kinds of neuroses, paranoia, and other mental illnesses can be linked to sexuality.

SEXUAL HARMONY IMPROVES THE QUALITY OF LIFE

Tantrics say that when your sexual life is more harmonious, it affects all aspects of your life. You become more optimistic, positive, cheerful, relaxed, and happy – all because you have good sex. It affects our egos. When men are not sexually satisfied and are not successful as lovers, they compensate for that by acting out, sometimes in very cruel ways (becoming dictatorial types or despicable bosses) or simply by exhibiting passive-aggressive or antisocial behavior, without even being aware of it. Some modern conditions such as Attention Deficit Disorder (ADD) can be linked to this same cause and probably, if we dig deep enough, similar connections exist for other illnesses. And this is what Freud claimed as well, actually, linking dreams to sexual wishes or frustrations. In his own words: "We have already asserted elsewhere that dreams which are conspicuously innocent invariably embody coarse erotic wishes, and we might confirm this by means of numerous fresh examples. But many dreams which appear indifferent, and which would never be suspected of any particular significance, can be traced back, after analysis, to unmistakably sexual wish-feelings, which are often of an unexpected nature." (From *Dream Psychology: Psychoanalysis for Beginners*, 1921)

When people start applying tantric principles in their lives, they start to see that everything in the universe is connected. The butterfly effect is real. If everything is connected to everything, sex is connected to everything too. Understanding that, you will see your life improve. A woman who is told by her partner that she is a good lover will walk around with a smile from ear to ear, suddenly with time to listen to others, and more patience. Men, too, will become less aggressive and more understanding, expressing love and compassion more easily.

❀ When practicing Tantra with my partner I feel like a priority, like *alpha* and *omega*, like the beginning and end and endlessness. It's an unfamiliar feeling for the mind when instead of concentrating on myself (both people striving for their own pleasure, as often happens between men and women), the predominant wish is to give everything for the partner to be happy.

I feel safe because I know with every cell in my body and every piece of my soul that I am protected. I can let go of all the everyday things, allowing myself to be taken along with the different feelings that arise during the practice. It's like flying in an endless sky, a feeling that I'm free to move in whatever direction and my partner is always with me; I don't fall!

I feel like I'm new every time. Every time differs from the last time, even if the difference is only in small nuances. The developments during the practice allow me to experience new sensations, even in previously familiar situations. I am happy to be with a partner who makes even very hard discoveries accomplishable. He has belief when I lose mine, and he has the confidence to share with me when I'm doubtful.

— *Kristina*

A MIRACLE PILL FOR RELATIONSHIP PROBLEMS

Of course Tantra has great, total, and sometimes even categorical effects on relationships. So many relationship problems and issues resolve by themselves – with no need to set ground rules for the toilet seat or who does the dishes – because harmonious sex has solved the friction in the relationship down to these petty levels. Many modern therapies recommend introducing imagination and playing with toys and roles to resolve relationship problems. But this is not a deep or long-lasting solution. Instead, it actually starts a vicious circle, which can be traced back to looking for answers in the wrong places. When a couple believes they made some progress, only to discover that sexuality becomes flat again, in some cases this even leads to an obsession with fantasy and a loss of energy.

Do you remember when you were in elementary school and one day there was a special presentation on sexual education? Do you remember what you were taught in that class? In many countries in the world – and I have visited many – most people admitted that the class was very superficial and the knowledge given was almost a cartoonish approach to biology and mating.

In a typical scenario, a teacher stands before the class and says, "Today we're going to talk about sex." Most kids get embarrassed and start laughing nervously. The teacher shows a picture of a man's penis and woman's vagina and explains that if a man and woman are sexually attracted to each other, the man gets an erection, penetrates the woman's vagina, sperm comes out and, if the egg is fertilized, nine months later a baby will be born. If you don't want sexually transmitted diseases or babies (yet), better use a condom. End of class. Can this be considered a serious guide to sexuality? No. The Kinsey Reports, studies conducted by Masters and Johnson, and other research have tried to go a bit deeper, but we still find that modern sexology revolves around sex approached from a physiological or biological standpoint.

Here is where the problems start. Sex cannot be reduced to biological or physiological studies, male and female anatomies, and sexual organs as merely organs of reproduction – all of this is very limiting. As a result, couples try to deal with their sexual disappointments by using aphrodisiacs or vitality enhancers like Viagra (which combats impotence), and they begin to view sex as an outlet for stress reduction.

MODERN MEN ARE TOO QUICK

Men approach sexuality in a very competitive, masculine manner. When a man is young, he discovers sexuality through masturbation, which takes the form of immediate relief, a race to quick pleasure and orgasm. He ejaculates, then leaves it behind and moves on to doing something else…. This is why for many males the sexual encounter is very short – sometimes only 20 seconds, which is still considered by some to be enough!

If a man engages in the sex act just once without emitting semen, then his vital essence will become strong. If he does so twice, his hearing and vision will become very clear. If three times, all bodily diseases will disappear. If four times, an inner peace will become attached to his spirit. If five times, then his blood circulation will be greatly improved. If six times, his loins will become very strong. If seven times, his thighs and buttocks will increase their power. If eight times, his whole body will become shining and radiant. If nine times, his life expectancy will increase.
— Yi-Fang-Pi-Chuch

Women's anatomy and psychology are very different, although women, too, discover masturbation at quite a young age. In many societies up to 20 or 30 percent of women never really experience an orgasm. Of course, the rest do, but often only through self-stimulation and not with a partner. Women's sexual organs are internal, which means they need more time to become aroused. Women also crave a psychological and emotional aspect in their lovemaking. They need to feel admired, desired, and loved. They need more foreplay and pleasure that increases gradually prior to lovemaking. Another important point is the need for a woman to be able to accept and love herself. That means accepting her body and not comparing it to the unrealistic and many times photoshopped images in the media and also learning to forgive and love herself in the innermost part of her being.

❀ Tantric knowledge has fundamentally changed my understanding of myself as a woman and my sexuality. ...Before getting to know Tantra I was sure that I was one of the women who simply didn't experience vaginal orgasms. I thought women were sexually divided into two: some only experience clitoral orgasms and others "are able" to experience deeper orgasms. It did not occur to me to contemplate that maybe everyone is able to have deeper experiences and to search for the reasons or blockages preventing it. Now it is clear to me that I have no disability, that I am perfect in every sense. Now I have experienced deeper orgasms and women's ejaculation, which I had thought I surely was not able to experience. When practicing Tantra with a tantric man I feel myself like a real goddess who is in the most loving and reliable hands in the universe! I feel I am loved unconditionally and unselfishly, that the goal of the man is to give me as much pleasure and tenderness as possible. I also feel that people look at me as a goddess – with respect and dignity. Discovering Tantra is one of the most wonderful discoveries in my life so far.

— *Tiina*

WHAT HAPPENED TO ALL THE PASSION?

Let's discuss porn for a minute. When women watch pornography, they need to perceive an unfolding story. For men, meanwhile, it's enough if the actress has big breasts and there's action – the story is almost irrelevant. These two different approaches to sex demonstrate an incompatibility on one level.

We know that when we meet a new person, there is inherently something like a very strong aphrodisiac involved. But when the initial infatuation fades – at the six-month to three-year mark, usually – daily life takes over and both start to experience sexual boredom. The man does not show the same passion toward the woman as he once did – frustration, anger, and anxiety start to manifest. The woman complains often that, "Before we were having sex everywhere, and six months later my partner is sitting on the couch with a beer, watching TV. I could walk around the house naked and he wouldn't even care…." This by the way, works both ways, unfortunately. Many times men also say that women used to be "goers" who were very willing and adventurous sexually, but once they settled into the security of a relationship, they suddenly lost their interest in sex and started withholding it from their partners.

This is what happens when our education is focused only on the physiological approach to sex. The tantric approach takes us out of this situation and teaches us how to sustain passion. In recognizing that we have a certain amount of sexual energy, *ojas* Shakti, in our being, we can learn to control it and use it wisely, maintaining our sexual passion.

Sexual energy is not just hormones and biological chemicals. It is an electrical field which can be increased. We can enhance our sexual magnetism, making it deeper and more powerful as time goes by. Tantra teaches us the basic techniques to help conserve that special energy, helping us in the process learn to solve the problems of modern sexology.

EXERCISE: A SIMPLE PRACTICE FOR INCREASING SEXUAL MAGNETISM AND PASSION

As partners in a couple, you should have a short discussion in which you both agree that, for the time being, orgasm will not be the purpose of your sexual union. Rather, you will take regular sex off the plate until further notice, making your objectives only to give pleasure to one another and allow yourselves to receive pleasure. The idea is not to be goal-oriented or too focused on the orgasm, but rather to be focused on giving and surrender. Learn to enjoy the process instead of obsessing over the objective and you'll be surprised to find out that the passion and chemistry enhance a lot.

Begin with tantric massage (or simply an oil massage,

for those who do not have tantric massage training). Focus on the sensations of pleasure with no urgency whatsoever. Use your sense of touch, your mouth, or any other body-to-body sensations. However, the emphasis in this practice is different in that you focus on the contact itself and not rushing through it, which is why there are no special step-by-step instructions or protocols. Do what you like anyway but with the right attitude. Take your time and let go of any "animalistic desires for climax." Explore each other's bodies and massage gently until both of you are fully aroused; it's essential that the woman be very aroused and vibrating. Conclude the session with no explosion, no ejaculation, and no climax; instead both of you should sweetly savor the joy of giving you just shared together and treasure the sensations pulsating inside you.

Once the session has concluded, it is advisable that both of you do a session of *Hatha Yoga* in order to sublimate the sexual arousal (move them up in the body) that resulted from the massage.

Continue with these tantric or sensual massage sessions for a minimum of three weeks and then notice the magnetism and attraction that has developed between the two of you. At this point it is recommended that you seek out a Tantra workshop or teacher to guide you to the next level of building the relationship and passion.

VIII

TANTRIC RELATIONSHIPS

A high percentage of couples today develop serious relationship problems. We can just look at the divorce rate worldwide, which unfortunately is trending up not only in more puritanical countries but also in more open societies. Partners often develop a relationship and commit to it in the form of a marriage, but after a while (years or, in some cases, only months) they become disappointed, losing hope for a fulfilling and satisfying relationship, and choose to divorce. In many cases, partners even concurrently begin to explore sexually outside the relationship, thinking that may solve the problem, but normally it doesn't. The new relationship is rarely satisfying either and, in the meantime, the infidelity – whether or not it has been revealed – has undoubtedly become a damaging factor in the primary relationship, inducing a loss of trust and connection. For partners who conclude that their relationship has failed (often repeatedly) the question may pop up: "I don't know what's wrong with me. Do I just keep choosing the wrong kind of person?"

Relationship problems often occur at a level beyond the sexual level. **Most relationships get their spark from attraction**. When sexual passion dies out, the partners begin to realize they do not have much in common and no longer have the affinity to be in a relationship after all. Every human being has the deep need to find a partner, to feel support, love, and the intimacy and connection that brings them happiness. Of course, they seek a regular lovemaking partner too. From a tantric standpoint a relationship is a way to develop spiritually and it is seen as the path to enlightenment. However, some people may not want this from their relationships – they seek mainly companionship and sexual fulfillment.

When my beloved returns to the house, I shall make my
body into a Temple of Gladness. Offering this body as
an altar of joy, my let-down hair will sweep it clean.
Then my beloved will consecrate this temple.
— Vaisnav Baul Song

THE MAGICAL DANCE OF SHIVA AND SHAKTI

A beautiful metaphor for the divine couple of Shiva and Shakti exists within the *devadasi* tradition of temple dancers. At many tantric temples, which have existed throughout the history of India, people would go to pray and worship the unification of male and female, symbolized in the *shivalingam*. In all temples you can find a statue of this symbol – a phallus, or *lingam*, rising from the middle of a *yoni*, representing the cosmic vagina, a symbol of the union of the supreme male and female principles. The famous *devadasi* temple dancers were tantric practitioners who learned and taught tantric dance. They did *Hatha Yoga* and *Kundalini Yoga* regularly, took care of their diet, and practiced tantric sex – sometimes with multiple partners – as part of their spiritual path.

From time to time those *devadasis* would go and perform a dance in a village or before the king and, while dancing, performing a very special set of movements, they would enter an ecstatic state and exemplify a specific energy of the Goddess. If they danced in front of an audience, that audience would literally see the consort of Shiva dancing in front of them, sanctifying the place with divine energy, bringing the divine into their daily lives, so total was their manifestation of the Goddess and devotion to Shiva.

The divine couple is the tantric ideal: a union, a marriage of opposites, an earthly manifestation of the supreme masculine (Shiva) and cosmic feminine (Shakti), whose lovemaking brought about the universe. Shakti is the feminine, primordial energy, while Shiva is both the ultimate *Vira* and pure consciousness, awareness, the center of existence. According to Tantra, Shiva is consciousness and by himself he does not have power. In the dynamics of Tantra, Shiva must have Shakti, and vice versa. Shiva without Shakti is nothing – there is consciousness but no manifestation, no energy. Shiva without Shakti is *shava*, which means a corpse. Without Shiva, Shakti does not reach pleasure, and energy is uncontrolled and chaotic, like a hurricane that destroys a whole city, an energy which has no directed purpose. When Shakti has Shiva, her energy is guided by consciousness, and she is satisfied. From a metaphysical viewpoint the union of the masculine and feminine is necessary for wholeness. Together they complete each other and reach perfect union and higher levels of consciousness.

These beautiful ideals manifest in the daily life of the average person. Many women probably don't even realize that when they have a masculine partner who exhibits the quality of centeredness, her needs are being met and she can from a place of fulfillment also satisfy her partner. The man feels she is working with him, supporting him, and giving him what he needs. **A man and woman need to develop a relationship in which an energetic balance is reached**, fulfilling their needs as individuals and partners.

I used to look for possibilities to energize my man, to fill him with love. Tantra saved our relationship. A tantric relationship is the only way to be – to live, to move on, and to communicate in a loving way – the only one that has ever existed. Only dedication and attention toward the woman open all channels and can offer the man a unique experience of energetic orgasm between each other's fields. This is powerful and very beautiful, indescribable in words – the best gift a woman can give to her man. A tantric partner enables the woman to really love and feel like a woman – full of abundance.

We have grown close to the ideal of real love. We attend tantric nights and there is now no sting in the heart when I see my dear man with other women. This situation has only occurred by learning to trust. Tantra has strongly influenced the level of respect between us. Angry energies have dissolved and been replaced by trust. There are fewer conflicts in the relationship and more heart and balance.

Tantra has brought significant changes in our relationship in multiple ways. We look each other in the eyes more often and more deeply, [and] we take each other's individuality into account. The bedroom's atmosphere begins even in the kitchen. Tantra has brought unconditional love into our lives. The relationship now flows by loving peacefully, with pressures forgotten. The most important aspect Tantra has brought into our relationship is energetics.

— *Ülle*

TANTRA IS FOREMOST A PATH OF LOVE

In Tantra, a relationship must be based on one very important thing: true love. True love can be misunderstood a lot due to the modern celebration of the ego, distortion in the media, Hollywood movies, and magazines, where "love" is expressed as clingy, jealous, passionate behavior totally conditioned on reciprocity. Love is understood to-day as a salad – a mix between love, sex, lust, jealousy, and a lot of other emotions – a confusing, unstable mix, which can resemble a soap opera as it unfolds in real life.

Your heart is the size of an ocean.
Go find yourself in its hidden depths.
— Rumi

True love in Tantra is considered to be pure. **If it is not pure, it is not real**. Yes, this is a very idealistic approach, but tantrics believe in idealism. True love is like divine love, the love between gods – unconditional, devoted, and as archetypal as the love seen in fairytales. Such love is something that everybody aspires for – a love that en-dures through the difficulties and obstacles of life, re-maining pure and deep, and lasting possibly even until our next reincarnation…. This kind of true love is so dif-ficult to realize because people are not willing to make the effort needed to sustain it.

Tantrics say that love is never real unless it is free. If you try to contain love with rules and regulations, then it is not love anymore – it's a type of contract. It is difficult for many to consider an alternative to the world in which love exists when a man and woman get married, have children, and live within a structured relationship that prescribes certain behavior, and so on. But what if you went on a vacation and fell in love with somebody? Does it mean you would suddenly love your current partner less? Are you then a criminal? Do you have a problem that means you should be ashamed of yourself? If you think so, ask yourself why? If love in its concept is so beautiful, why can't we fully accept its infinite and un-contained nature? We can't because social rules exist that encourage being "normal," and if you don't follow those rules, it's presumed that something is wrong with you. This kind of approach chokes love.

Many relationships find themselves in trouble these days. If you look at the divorce rate in most countries today compared to 50 years ago or further back in history, it is incredible! All over the world, divorce rates have increased substantially over the last century. For example, in the United States in the 1950s the divorce rate was 26 percent, but by 1985 it had grown to a whopping 50 percent, a rate close to that seen today. (See Historical Divorce Rate Statistics by attorney Audrey M. Jones.) Some people actually applaud, pointing out that this shows progress – people are freer and can do what they want, leaving unhappy relationships. But if it is so amazing, then where is the happiness? By no means are we implying here that in earlier times, people were not experiencing problems in relationships. Indeed, society may have been more constricting in its rules and some people may have even been forced to marry and live out an unhappy life in a relationship they did not want due to social or religious mores at the time. Nevertheless, there is an obvious worrisome trend in modern relationships that indicates a real problem. I have met personally hundreds and hundreds of people who complain about the fact that they are not happy in their relationships. This is due to a basic lack of understanding about true love.

The only way is: love in, ego out. Love cannot work otherwise. Tantrics say that real love and relationships manifest themselves purely from the heart and accept the partner in all his or her aspects. True love is forgiveness without remembering faults, peacefulness without promoting anger, selflessness rather than selfishness, and above all not reveling in jealousy and possessiveness but rather rejoicing in the other's happiness.

The Bible elegantly defines love in Corinthians 13:4-8: **Love is patient, love is kind. It does not envy, it does not boast, it is not proud. It is not rude, it is not self-seeking, it is not easily angered, it keeps no record of wrongs. Love does not delight in evil but rejoices with the truth. It always protects, always trusts, always hopes, always perseveres. Love never fails. ...**

Love is the most important thing. It is the food of life, helping us truly achieve happiness. Everybody wants it, but most of the time the ego steps in and makes a mess. Now that I have discussed love a little bit, if we put love in the context of relationships, then asking whether tantrics believe in monogamy or open relationships becomes an irrelevant question. It is not about open or closed relationships – it is about love. Do you love truly or not? Because if you don't love truly, then does it really matter if you have an open or closed relationship? If there is no true love, the relationship will not work. Without love it is more like business-minded cooperation: Two people have a contract for exclusive sex, they create some children together, they own property together, and it works well, like a company. If that works for them, I respect that, but in that case no one can be upset if love is missing, because reality responds to the space given to our priorities in life.

To be clear, we are not saying here that love cannot be true and real in a closed relationship with fidelity. I know tantric couples who are exclusive and have wonderfully true relationships. Our point here is that as much as both options (open or closed relationships) are acceptable in Tantra, the condition of love being true, real, and without ego is absolutely necessary.

If you want love and the magic it brings, love cannot obey any rules. Partners who experience true love may seem crazy to others, foolishly looking into each other's eyes for hours. **When you are in love you are transported suddenly to another level of consciousness**. So you must follow you heart on this question, whether you are satisfied and happy with an open or closed relationship. It's for each person to decide individually. I know tantric couples personally who are in closed relationships and have reached very deep and wonderful levels in their relationship together. They are very happily in love and that is the bottom line. On the other hand, I also know tantrics who have two or three lovers, and maybe their lovers have other lovers if they are involved in a tantric community whose members accept openness in relationships. And they truly love each of their lovers, experiencing a completely fulfilling, beautiful, and wonderful relationship with each, also in deep love. There is no jealousy or anger. If jealousy arises, they deal with it in a mature way, with an understanding of the toxic nature of this emotion, and they remedy their trust in each other with meditation, Yoga practice, and talking through the issues. They remove it by confronting it, which means confronting the ego and its insecurities. Open tantric relationships often put their participants on a "fast track" of evolution, because it is a more profound experience to confront and tackle these disempowered feelings until they are resolved in your being than to hope you can avoid dealing with the feelings by avoiding situations in which these feelings arise.

CONFRONTING THE EGO
AND ITS MOST EVIDENT ASPECT – JEALOUSY

Today for many people jealousy is a sign of love. You see these two intertwined everywhere – in movies, at parties, etc. A couple goes to a party and a woman starts to believe that her man is not paying enough attention to her. What to do? She goes off and starts flirting with someone else to stir up her partner's jealousy. And when the jealousy strikes, she is happy because she feels that her partner loves her. **Jealousy is not a sign of love; it is a sign of love dying. It is the opposite of love. From a tantric point of view, jealousy is a poison and for this reason tantrics take dealing with jealousy very seriously. They consider jealousy to be an impurity that needs to be removed.**

We can implore a tantric teacher or therapist to help us, to tell us what we need to do. However, many people are not aware of their own ego, which can form an obstacle on the path of transformation. The first step is to be humble enough to acknowledge that we do not know everything. Some people simply will not ask for help. But if you have the courage to ask, only then will you receive and manage to realize by yourself where your blockages exist. Tantra offers techniques to heal ourselves and remove these blockages. Once you learn them, you will attract a different kind of person and notice that your relationships *can and do* change. If you are already in a relationship, you can invite a dynamic of positive change to be present there as well. Techniques that help in these cases are usually those that open up the heart chakra and meditation techniques that help us to overcome old mental programming and negative habits.

As people, we often have the tendency to blame the other in conflicts or when problems arise, always looking outwardly instead of inwardly to resolve issues of responsibility in our lives. Looking from an objective perspective, we can see that this is an immature approach. Similarly we may be unwilling to make efforts if things don't go entirely our way. If we don't like the game, we quit. Commitment – what's that? We go into relationships, but if we don't like them, we get out. However, this can reflect a very self-absorbed approach to life. Commitment is something much bigger. One plus one doesn't always equal two. When we discuss human potential, it can equal 10.

It is a magical thing to see couples surpass their jealousy, loving and supporting each other no matter what, even (and especially) within open relationships. It is at this point that freedom is truly present in the relationship and love finds the space to breathe.

MONO OR POLY? SHARING TANTRA WITH ONE OR SEVERAL LOVERS

Often when people hear about Tantra, they envision that it involves a license for free, kinky sex, exotic sex in wild positions, some swingers' clubs with orgies, or sexual adventurers enraptured by carnal desires. Certainly Tantra can be wild, but all of these ideas form the wrong impression, leaving out Tantra's entire spiritual basis and reducing sex to sport, and an impersonal one at that. Tantra may be so misunderstood due to the fact that many commonly misidentify themselves as tantrics in society; some people may be entirely unspiritual and have no understanding or knowledge at all about Tantra, but they claim to be tantrics and engage in these activities… which has in places tarnished the reputation of Tantra.

Some tantrics find it very satisfying to discover the universe of Shakti and Shiva with one person, whereas others feel their heart as open enough to share this journey with several partners. According to Tantra, **love is infinite** and loving two partners (or even more) equally and deeply is not only real but is also the only acceptable option for some. For these tantrics, a lifetime of withholding the physical demonstration of love from loved ones in the name of "fidelity," a somehow bourgeois idea, is simply

Somananda

Somananda's guru and teacher, Swami Vivekananda Saraswati

The shivalingam, a sacred tantric symbol, can be found in temples across India. It symbolizes the cosmic union of the masculine and feminine.

Somananda stands on the bank of the Ganges River in the sacred city of Rishikesh, India. It was here that his tantric journey began in 1999.

A beautiful ashram garden in Rishikesh fills up annually with pilgrims during the pilgrimage season.

International Yoga Festival 2012

Spiritual statues can be seen all over Rishikesh. Here a gate depicts a scene from the Bhagavad-Gita, *with a Shiva statue in the background.*

One of the thousands of statues and figurines featured among the erotic temples in Khajuraho, India. This temple, approximately 1,000 years old, still stands today.

Somananda presents a Tantra workshop at the Agama Yoga School in Thailand.

While in Estonia, Somananda often gives lectures to business groups or university students.

Somananda leads a class at Bhairava Yoga, the school he founded in 2010 in Estonia.

Swami Vivekananda Saraswati lectures at the 2013 International Tantra Festival in Estonia, an initiative started by Somananda.

Somananda's daily practices include meditation for union with the highest consciousness and tantric principle, Shiva.

inauthentic. There is no judgment that one approach supersedes the other; both are beautiful and acceptable. In one-on-one relationships, partners must be appreciated as the divine beings they are and not regarded without respect or simply as financial providers. The tantrics say that if you understand these high principles before going into a relationship, you must look deeply within yourself and see what you bring to the relationship. Like attracts like; if you are an angry and aggressive person, you will attract that as well. If a woman carries within her some trauma from the past, sexual dysfunctions, etc., she is subconsciously broadcasting that with her resonance, body language, choice of words, and facial expressions. And if a woman has a victim mentality, she will attract a predatory type of partner. We need to recognize that the law of resonance applies even at this level and understand what is going on within us energetically, too As much as we emphasized earlier the value of commitment in relationships and engaging in it for the right reasons, we also find that in some cases the opposite is necessary. Today many partners stay together for the wrong reasons, preferring to remain in unhappy relationships rather than making a change and, if need be, ending a relationship in order to find happiness and grow without the fear of being single temporarily (or even for long periods of time). It is well known that in most societies, individuals experience the general pressure to cultivate a family and it seems very irresponsible or problematic if one chooses a path that does not fit with social norms. This pressure in many cases may push us to make the wrong choices.

A similar pressure is at work socially pushing us to choose monogamy as the only acceptable relationship model. It does take a great deal of maturity and courage to choose open relationships, as well as a commitment to personal evolution. Unlike being single, where your friends will applaud your sexual liberation, open relationships are different. People judge that either you must not care about your partner if you are willing to share him or her or you must not care about yourself if you are willing to give up your exclusive status…. Honestly, all those in open relationships face a test in challenging the status quo, entering a relationship without letting eons of religious and social conditioning get in the way of love. It's important to understand that you will be tested, because you are pushing the envelope. When your fortitude feels low, you can remind yourself that no one said it would be easy!

Open relationships often involve challenges but such relationships reward the partners with hearts that grow much faster, spirits that expand due to generosity, giving, and surrender, courage that is strengthened every single day, and love that is true. Love is infinite. Let your love be infinite no matter which type of relationship you choose.

Love one another, but make not a bond of love:
Let it rather be a moving sea between the shores of your souls.
— Kahlil Gibran

GUIDE YOUR SHAKTI TO THE HEART

In the tantric experience, the sexual energy can bounce you in any direction as a drug might. Having ordinary sex and indulging an explosive orgasm with its concurrent loss of sexual energy is somewhat similar to taking drugs: You've let chemicals run loose in your brain, neurons explode wildly, and you have a chaotic experience. While such an experience may be "fun" or a "bad trip," depending who you are, at the end of the day it all comes down to the same bottom line: When approaching powerful energy in an uncontrolled manner, results are always unpredictable. The lucky ones have great sex and relationships and we call them just that – lucky. The others experience shades of gray.

But by preparing the body and mind and using transfiguration, sex itself is done with awareness and the sexual energy blooms before you. Instead of letting it run chaotically, you guide it where you want it to go. Tantra is like a scientific, well-trodden path, a process that has been developed to such a degree of precision that it is almost mathematical.

The first main objective of the tantric practice is to guide the awakened sexual energy toward the heart chakra. This is not a mystical concept or some touchy-feely misguided New Age wish about "reaching for love." This chakra center is considered in Tantra an important energy center and a level of consciousness that not only leads human beings to higher spiritual accomplishments, but also can have a transformational effect on their lives, bringing harmony, true love, and much more. Thus tantric practitioners consider it very valuable to focus the energy at the level of the heart in tantric sexuality.

THE PROCESS OF TRANSMUTATION AND SUBLIMATION

By guiding your Shakti to the heart, the energy in that area starts expanding. The love that is suddenly created is love of a true kind – real and unconditional, not a "love" contaminated by misguided feelings and lust, dominated by the ego. This process of energy transmutation is a big part of the tantric sexual teachings and it comes hand-in-hand with the concept of sublimation, which is the channeling of transmuted energies to the higher levels of the being. The sexual energy is raw and not refined, but thanks to special techniques in Tantra for transmuting this enegy, using a kind of inner heat, the energies are transmuted and then led upward to the higher levels. In a way it is almost like the process of refining crude oil – with a process involving heat, it transforms from a thick, sticky liquid into a nearly clear, high-octane gasoline for use in cars. In the same way, we guide the raw sexual potential upward to the first stop amidst the higher levels of the being, the heart chakra. This is the seat of pure and true love, uncontaminated by jealousy and expectations. Isn't such love everybody's dream, that which all couples aspire for? Sometimes if you make a cake from scratch, it turns out perfectly. However, the other 99 percent of the time, if you don't follow a recipe, you simply won't succeed. Approaching sex without knowledge or awareness is also a kind of gamble. Tantra brings the recipe of success to the sexual union.

PRACTICAL EXERCISE FOR COUPLES: TRANSMUTATION AND SUBLIMATION OF THE SEXUAL ENERGY

Sit together in front of each other on a Yoga mat or bed in a place where you won't be disturbed. You can play some soft, harmonious music in the background. Look into each other's eyes for at least five minutes while holding hands. Then close your eyes and start breathing deeply. Try to breathe mostly from the abdominal area, with slow and deep breaths, while you are both fully relaxed.

Using your mind, concentrate to visualize a flame, like a candle flame lighting up and burning in the area of your navel. Feel how the heat is increasing gently. Now add a few strong exhalations through the nose and then resume normal deep breathing. Repeat this a few times.

After about 10 minutes you will both notice an increase of inner heat and may even begin to perspire.

This is a good sign. Feel how the sexual energy in the area of your loins begins to become more light and subtle while it is moving upward in your body. Once you begin to feel this, direct this feeling to the area of your heart center, in the middle of your chest.

For the last five or 10 minutes of this exercise, each of you should focus both in the area of the heart center and simultaneously to feel an intimate connection with the other at the level of the heart.

At this point you can conclude and hug each other.

IS IT POSSIBLE TO BE GAY AND TANTRIC?

This question comes up in many of my workshops, especially as the social acceptance of gay relationships has become more common and marriage equality is gaining traction around the world. Let's put it this way, in its original texts the tantric tradition did not provide any information on tantric relationships within the same gender. We know that gay relationships existed in ancient times, but no tantric teachings were given that specifically addressed gay and lesbian partners.

Modern tantrics adapt. They take the tantric knowledge they have and combine it with their spiritual discrimination and maturity to reach the best approach they can. It is therefore possible for gays and lesbians to have tantric relationships and experience tantric sexuality. There are always couples who head in that direction, even some of my students among them. I simply give them the knowledge about energy – because energy is energy and it applies to every person, no matter what their sexual orientation is.

Within a gay relationship, the tantric sexual practices – once learned – should be applied in the spirit of the original tantric teachings. This means that, first of all, each partner must learn to control their sexual energy, making efforts with the practices of Tantra; it is the same whether we speak of gay or straight relationships. For gay couples, Tantra should work at least to a certain degree. If difficulties are encountered, gay tantric practitioners can ask for support from their teacher and, if they are open and receptive to this support, eventually their tantric practice should be as successful as it is for heterosexual couples.

HOW TO GET GOING ON THE TANTRIC TRAIL

The tantric path is a long and diversified road. It is important that the body is ready for the tantric training. Just as we need to raise our energetic frequency, to get started successfully, it's also necessary to enhance our level of purity and prepare ourselves emotionally and mentally with certain practices.

Tantra views the sexual energy in an unconventional way. For most people the sexual energy is very basic, understood as a means to reach intimacy and as a biological or physiological force that can relieve stress and provide some relaxation. In Tantra this is also true, but the reality goes much further than that. Tantric couples will approach lovemaking in a much slower and more conscious way. They take care of their diet, purifying themselves and their bodies, reducing toxins in their lives so that energy can move more freely and easily within them. Most likely if both are practicing Tantra they will meditate regularly; this is a very vast part of Tantra, as it is in many other traditions.

For tantrics, meditation is a way of harmonizing emotions and cleansing the mind, eliminating obsessive factors, negative thoughts, and also karmic baggage. Regular meditation leads partners to approach their sexuality with fewer unrealistic expectations and without runaway imagination, thus generally in a more mature way. The sexual act itself does not start before the partners in a tantric couple transfigure each other as Shiva and Shakti.

Next, there are tantric methods for purifying not only our chakras, but also the thinking process and emotional structure. Once you have begun to follow a regimen of purification, you will notice a change in your relationships that is initially evidenced by better communication and interaction with those around you. However, beware that this is exactly the crossroads where you are likely to confront your ego: "It feels like I am making all the tantric efforts and my partner does not seem to try – he just stays the same. It doesn't seem fair – maybe I should stop my efforts too!" It's obvious to see that this kind of thinking pattern doesn't take you very far.

Tantric sexuality and training can create challenges. Relationships can definitely grow, becoming much more solid. But the process that takes a relationship to the next level – which everybody aspires for – is not necessarily easy. I remember when I spent time at tantric camps with thousands of people from various countries and I spoke to others there about the challenges and problems I was facing at the time in my tantric relationship. I was amazed to discover that within a tantric relationship in such tantric environments, partners can develop the relationship at a much faster rate than in so-called everyday life. I learned that many tantric couples notice that their relationship faces challenges, even in its early stages, which in a normal environment would be faced only years later. In other words, the evolution of the relationship is speeded up, maturing and developing much more quickly than under ordinary conditions. In a tantric environment a relationship is tested in a way that may produce exponential growth, showing sometimes in one year the growth a normal relationship would see in 10.

When looking back, many experiences that I used to regard as science fiction have become true and I have enjoyed it. My own attitude has changed (also toward myself), including that preconceptions and ego have subsided. All this has made me more self-confident and open. A readiness to move on and experience something new has grown in me, I'm more willing to let go of control and just allow things to happen, and the list goes on. My body has become more sensitive. The practices give a gradual awakening. It seems as though my body had been asleep before and now it slowly awakens in small stages. I can only say it's a wonderful experience….

The most important change that Tantra has brought into my life is the emergence of awareness – knowing is added to feeling, of how, why, and when something goes on in or around me. By getting to know myself better I can also understand others better, which makes all communication more balanced, meaningful, deeper, and also happier and harmonious, reducing excessive emotions and offering warmth and immediacy, especially in close relationships, in family. It's almost like every woman's dream….

I can feel joy and be happy over small things: an open gate when coming home, warm soup when stepping inside, a light left on for those arriving late, a smile, peaceful silence while being together, Sunday morning bustle in the kitchen, a friendly handshake, etc. It seems that the inner peace and happiness which Tantra has brought into my life are quite related and they make each day valuable, a day worth living. Tantra has brought more moments in my life that I wish for so much – moments when I'm happy!

— *Kristina*

Transfiguration is one of the biggest and most important tantric teachings. It is considered to be both method and objective in Tantra, **changing our view of reality**. And not only changing the external view, **but also creating a very poetic inner view of reality**. It may have paranormal or even magical effects. This tantric practice can be done with a partner or applied to an environment – it can be brought to every aspect of life.

Transfiguration is not actually optional in a tantric relationship; it is fundamental and essential. It is a sophisticated method of beautifying and sprinkling magic on each other and the environment around us. Partners simply consciously adjust their mental perceptions of each other, positively idealizing each other as divine beings, which elevates the frequency of the sexual union and transforms it from instinctual copulation into sacred union. According to Tantra, when attraction is greatly enhanced, desire is taken to an exponential degree on purpose, control and passion are increased, and the need to unite becomes almost a cry of the soul. That creates a state in which sexual union is ecstatic. It is the embodiment of every human's nostalgic, deep need to experience sexuality as we have all dreamed in the core of our being.

In today's world, we are heavily brainwashed by Hollywood movies and women's magazines, which lead us to believe that sex is supposed to give us something magical – the pleasure of an orgasm which transports us into the clouds. In the reality that exists for most couples, sexual chemistry – while strong and fulfilling in its early stages – doesn't last indefinitely. It could take a few months or a year or more but, sooner or later, the attraction subsides, fading and becoming less compelling. On a conscious or subconscious level, many people are aware of this. Commonly, when couples have troubles, they ask: "Where did the magic and passion go? We had something good – what happened? How can we fix it?"

The description which follows can serve as an exercise in how to introduce transfiguration to your life; you are encouraged to read it, spend some time meditating on it, and then try to apply it. The simplest way to describe transfiguration is to try to understand how an artist or poet looks at the world. For example, compare how a doctor, engineer, and poet look at the naked body of the woman. What would each of them say? The doctor might observe the woman and say that her height is average, she looks relatively healthy and fit, and so on – analyzing the body as a doctor normally does. The engineer might say that the muscle tone is good, the proportions and angles can be evaluated – basically he would consider the mechanics of any object. But when the poet looks upon a woman's body, he would probably say something like:

Her eyes are like two lakes in the middle of the forest, her skin is soft like a river of milk, and her hips curve so beautifully, like dunes in the desert….

A dry and unimaginative person who doesn't understand poetic metaphor might say, "What is he talking about? Lakes in the forest? Do you know how lakes look in the forest? There is a lot of mud as well as many insects and frogs! What's the connection?" They can't see it. But the poet sees things in a different way, a kind of associated way. He sees beyond reality and makes connections which may sound strange or a bit crazy, and yet this is the vision that moves us.

When we think about what makes our hearts sing, it is the poet's view – a way of transforming reality. Suddenly we see the beauty and magic of everything around us. It is a little bit like being in love. When we see people in love, sometimes we think they have lost their minds. They are transfiguring the object of their love nonstop. And what do we all want? Love! The way to open our hearts to love is to learn how to transfigure. Authentic tantrics transfigure continuously, 24 hours a day – they cannot stop. It becomes a sort of natural state.

How do you learn *not* to stop love and magic and sexuality? Why is it so necessary in Tantra? With practice, transfiguration heightens the senses. It creates electricity in the air. It is like a couple in love – when they sit next to each other and touch each other, sparks fly. Why do many couples say that in the beginning of their relationship the sex was crazy and magical, but after a few months they lost it? It is because this electric chemistry was lost. And transfiguration teaches us how to have that all the time.

❧ We have participated in transfiguration rituals. I've felt myself very magically during the ritual, as if all veils and covers fall, and the primeval woman emerges with all that the Creator has created.

My partner felt the different kinds of femininity of each woman and sensed the beauty of every woman and girl (irrespective of the external beauty). Also in everyday life he started to see a young and desirable woman in every old lady by the road. He learned to look through the external and saw in the mind's eye, with physically open eyes, a young woman inside the old one. He got such an energizing experience from this and was happy for how this expanded his senses. It all happened to me the same way, only a bit more intensively. I saw auras around people and their soul-light shining from body apertures. The spirit is so big, it can't fit inside the body.

— *Ülle*

Transfiguration is also the secret to health, love, and happiness. It makes life incredible. When you transfigure your partner while making love, the experience is much more powerful. It affects reality, because reality is affected by our eyes, the way we look and see everything. It is said that beauty is in the eye of the beholder, but what does that really mean? It means that the way the world is revealed to you is directly related to the energy you invest in it, the way you choose to look at it, what you give to it, your attitude, state of mind, and emotions. In Tantra, we call this transfiguration – seeing the divine in the partner, in all aspects of life. This is the essence behind all we do in Tantra – making life divine…. This is about waking up inside. It is like falling in love. You hardly fall in love just by reading a book about somebody – you have to see the person physically and look into their eyes, and then things start happening. So to see how this can increase your happiness in life, it is recommended that you find a teacher or guru and study transfiguration.

WHAT ABOUT RITUALS?

Rituals are very common and popular, not only in Tantra but also in daily life. Even our habitual morning preparation for work – brushing our teeth, showering, and shaving – is a sort of ritual. Almost any teaching today which is spiritually oriented or religious involves rituals. All religions, for example, carry out rituals, because they have recognized that there is a power and potency to ceremony that allows a body of knowledge or set of special practices to sink deeply into the subconscious, where it can help guide conscious life even more effectively. Rituals seem very mysterious and magical, and many consider them exciting and fun. They can charge any room or hall with a special atmosphere.

Why is ritual such a classic thing in human history? Is it just because ancient people were primitive? They looked to the sky and because they couldn't explain the lightning and other natural phenomena, they created stories about gods, which led them to enact rituals honoring those gods, which made them feel protected. Sometimes there is a somewhat arrogant attitude toward rituals, as if they exist for less intelligent people. But in fact, rituals involve the science of magic. When you say magic, people automatically think of illusionist David Copperfield or fictional fantasy character Harry Potter, so we can see how the modern understanding has been shaped by cultural icons.

In fact, natural magic is a science which has existed among mankind for eons. The concept of magic is not something whimsical, like the cartoonish representations of magicians who say, "Abracadabra" and pull a rabbit out of a hat. Magic actually has a basis in understanding the laws of the universe. In ancient times, some traditions realized that nature has rules and principles which govern energy. From a causal standpoint – because there is a law of causality – action always brings reaction, equally and proportionally. This is well known in science as Newton's third law of motion, which states: "**For every action, there is an equal and opposite reaction.**"

So, when you look from the causal perspective at life, you realize there is always a chain of dominoes. Depending on this and that action, energy suddenly moves in a certain way. To the uninitiated it may look like magic in the same way that if you show up in an Aboriginal village with a flashlight, and the villagers have not learned about electricity, they will think a battery-operated "sun" is magic. Thus, magic originally was the understanding of some ways of operating in unison with certain laws of the universe. And in doing so, a whole system was created.

Likewise, religion was also presented similarly. If you look through all major religions on this planet from Hinduism to Christianity, Judaism to Buddhism, or any other, you will see ritual in practice. Most often, the members of a religious community are also invited to participate in certain rituals. The Catholic mass is a ritual, for example. The priest says certain prayers, walks in a specific way, uses special incense, and so on. Whatever he does, it is the sequence that the priest must not change. What he learned, he must do. It is the same for a rabbi in the Jewish tradition and for the Buddhist monk, who must follow hundreds of precepts and do specific chanting each fortnight. They cannot improvise; they must follow certain rules.

Why? Originally, rituals were designed by people who were enlightened and had reached high states of consciousness. They knew that rituals would help even those with work, families, and little or no time for religious practice to align their lives in more organized, spiritual ways. Let's face it – religions feature exoteric and not esoteric teachings, so they are meant for the masses and not for rare yogis who want to invest many hours daily in Yoga, meditation, and intense practice. We are talking about average people for whom time is limited, efforts are difficult, and the most they can usually do is to attend church on Sundays and recite some prayers. Rituals were designed exactly to meet this need to reach average people – "the masses" – on their own terms in ways that were much more accessible than the esoteric, advanced teachings common in educated circles.

The beauty of rituals is that they always work – but only if they are authentic. Today, in an environment influenced by New Age thinking – where information and misinformation must be diligently sifted to distinguish one from the other – experts seem to pop up left and right having created all kinds of fantastical new rituals. For example, one may have studied Reiki, like to do massage, had a dream about angels last night, so... she decides to light some candles, read some *mantras* from the Internet, wear white because it is cool and pure, and – voilà! – a ritual is born. This is very sweet indeed, but it is not a genuine ritual. A ritual is not a chaotic concept created by anyone with a good imagination. **It is created only by those who have reached high states of consciousness.** Such people understood that if they ask others to follow certain guidelines, energetic or spiritual results are guaranteed, even if the participants are completely ignorant spiritually. Rituals are in one way amazing, because they can bestow wonderful results. However, on the other hand, they represent the bottom drawer of spirituality. It is basic, rudimentary knowledge despite its extremely powerful effects.

🪷 A ritual fixes the most important knowledge that is hard to understand in everyday life. That we are all the children of the Creator, that we can "play" in this reality and at the same time feel connected to our deeper being, by helping to raise our vibration together. The better the participants are energetically tuned, the better the connection.

Rituals have strongly influenced the level of sexuality and connection between me and my partner. I can see pictures inside him in our common field, while being in myself.

— *Ülle*

In Tantra, we first always prepare the space for a ritual – cleaning it, lighting incense and candles, setting up an altar, etc. We also prepare ourselves, with bathing, anointment with sacred oils or perfumes, Yoga or meditation practice, etc. When we finally begin the ritual, we always perform a certain act called a *consecration*, which is a very high type of spiritual inner offering of the fruits of the action. In this technique from the *Karma Yoga* tradition, each participant, with eyes closed, focuses and offers the outcome or results of the ritual to the divine consciousness. This is a very elevated spiritual act of humbleness that connects participants with the divine levels of the universe. Transfiguration and other technical aspects of the ritual follow. A ritual normally ends with a meditation to seal and harmonize the energies, after which participants can move on to tantric sexual practices if they choose.

Tantric rituals involve energy because, as we recall, Tantra is the science of energy, Shakti. The purpose of ritual in Tantra is to bring a person into a certain state of being or resonance or, if the ritual is for more advanced practitioners, then to attain energetic results in the body, purifying the chakras, opening them up, and facilitating the movement of energy to reach high states of consciousness.

When dealing with people who are not advanced practitioners and have little time, Tantra has developed certain types of rituals different from those found in religious environments. They normally include some concentration, an understanding of the concept of transfiguration, and an understanding of how to move energy properly.

In many cases, tantric rituals are practiced in couples, which is the beautiful part. In this way, a couple can create balance between yin and yang, minus and plus, woman and man, female and male energies, and their polarity generally. Tantric rituals offer something powerful via the sexual energy, which is channeled through participants. Tantra additionally includes sexual rituals which take sexuality to a completely new level. These are not intended to be kinky, funny, weird, or used for spicing up the sex life in bored couples – which is what plenty of people already think Tantra represents. Rather, these rituals are powerful ceremonies designed to spiritually transform their participants.

Rituals can be performed for so many purposes, the list is almost endless. A person who is lucky enough to have the good karma to lose his or her virginity within the context of tantric lovemaking can participate in a specific ritual, usually planned by the experienced partner. A woman who will enter a relationship with another couple can participate in a ritual with the other woman beforehand or with the couple together. And of course, rituals are not necessarily sexual experiences; they can involve Yoga practices and techniques, meditation, visualization, etc., and can be done in groups of two, three, four, or more, up to hundreds of participants.

> *Out of Brahma, which is the Higher Self, came space;*
> *out of space, air; out of air, fire; out of fire, water;*
> *out of water, earth; out of earth, vegetation; out of*
> *vegetation, food; out of food, the body of all humanity.*
> — *Taittriya Upanishad*

The most well-known and grand ritual in Tantra is called *maithuna*, which is a very specific lovemaking ritual relying on elements from the natural world – earth, water, fire, air, and ether – to represent energy, Shakti, in a form of honor and worship. It sounds very basic, but simply the act of engaging the senses at this level and with the partner creates an energetic shift for the couple by the end of the ritual.

Tantra is very wise. Speaking in intellectual terms does not guarantee results. Feeling very satisfied mentally does not necessarily bring any true change or development physically, energetically, or at higher levels. However, if you know how to move your energy, results cannot be avoided. Of course very advanced techniques and methods exist for *kundalini* practice, including *mantras*, techniques of concentration and visualization, and many other powerful methods. Such methods can be found in yogic or tantric texts, for example, the renowned *Vijnana Bhairava Tantra*, which contains more than 100 powerful and practical meditation techniques for achieving high states of consciousness.

EXERCISE: THE *MAITHUNA* RITUAL

Before you can perform a *maithuna* ritual, a few items must be prepared in advance for use during the ritual. Some of the items may be more rare, but in this example I will mention these with options that are most easily obtained.

Items needed:

– A bowl filled with earth (from a garden for example)
– A bowl of sea water
– A candle
– A feather or smooth piece of silk cloth
  (or silk item of clothing)

Once the couple has prepared the space for the ritual (cleaning the room, arranging an altar, etc.) and themselves (by bathing and dressing in clean clothes), the next step is to purify the space energetically. This can be done by using incense and candles in the room, although some tantrics use mantras or other means.

Now the couple can begin the process of consecration (which may take 10 minutes or more). During this process of meditation, offering the fruits of the ritual to the divine is important.

Next the couple should sit facing each other and gaze into one another's eyes. This part of the ritual dedicated to eye gazing is very interiorizing and uplifting.

And now, step-by-step, the couple will use the items prepared in advance. First the partners take turns holding the bowl of earth to each other's nostrils to smell. This activates the earth element and root chakra.

Next, each takes a sip of the sea water to activate the water element and second chakra. Following this, each gazes into a candle flame for a few minutes to activate the fire element and third chakra. Next the silk or feather is used to gently touch each other, activating the air element and heart chakra.

For the last part, the woman stands before the man and removes all her clothes and he meditates on her naked body – the symbol of the fifth element – in a process that activates the ether element and throat chakra (this can be done for 10 minutes or more).

At this point the couple may choose to continue with tantric lovemaking itself or to stop here and meditate together for a while.

The process should be completed with a meditation giving thanks to the divine consciousness (or Shiva in the tantric tradition).

Alternatives:

These options are not necessary nor recommended for vegetarians or yogis, but in order to give complete information about this ritual they are mentioned here.

Some tantric schools suggest that other items be used:

– Earth: Parched wheat can be chewed in a small amount
– Water: Fish or radish can be chewed in a small amount
– Fire: Meat can be chewed in a small amount
– Air: Red wine can be tasted in a very small amount

IX

TANTRIC MASSAGE

While tantric sex generally balances and harmonizes its practitioners, sometimes it's possible that one partner may feel a bit overworked, uninterested in lovemaking, or just "off." In such cases, tantric massage can be of great help, relaxing the recipient and equalizing the energy levels of both partners. Energetically speaking, being "turned off" indicates low energy levels or some kind of blockage. When such a person receives a massage, a circuit of energy is restored, and he or she can simply receive, which can bring equilibrium. Tantric massage gives couples expanded options in their sexuality. They may find the massage – which is a wonderful form of intimacy – satisfies them enough by itself without proceeding to full-on sex. In addition, both may feel so deeply sexually aroused that suddenly sex becomes naturally the next step.

Tantric massage is a comprehensive form of body work, focusing intensely on the genitals of the partner within a holistic context. It must be learned from a teacher through personal instruction. I, for example, learned Ayurvedic massage from a teacher who taught North Indian Ayurvedic massage – a style quite different from South Indian Ayurvedic massage. I combined it with the tantric teachings I received from my teacher, Swami Vivekananda Saraswati, and my own extensive experience in Tantra to create a program of tantric massage which has proven very effective. I have been teaching tantric massage since 2009 in Europe and Asia.

❀ Tantric massage has given me self-confidence and opened me up. It has connected me to people with a similar mindset and helped me to find out what blocked my progress in life and made me unhappy. It has also presented me with solutions for solving my problems. Tantra has taught me what love is. It has changed my views on life and made me see that every moment is beautiful and every second is worth surrendering.

I see people around me who have become more self-confident, happier, and content with themselves after having experienced tantric massage. Tantric massage brings out the most genuine, beautiful, and warm emotions ….

— *Liina*

GENTLY UNLOCK YOUR PARTNER

One of the main objectives of tantric massage is to help your partner unlock areas of the body that are blocked or "stuck." This is achieved using a unique method of channeling enegy through your hands and body into the blocked points in your partner. For this, using the *marma* points from Ayurvedic massage is invaluable. Therefore, tantric massage is a kind of body work intended to help energy flow throughout the body, focusing especially on the body's vital points and specifically on those in the genitals and erogenous zones. A woman can help a man to circulate and sublimate the sexual energy, rather than storing it in the genitals, in order to control it better and experience multiple orgasms. For a woman, the same technique helps her unlock sexual blockages and learn to experience and achieve tantric orgasms. Many women hold a lot of stress, traumas, and other energetic and psychological blockages especially in the area of the genitals and G-spot. In fact, the *yoni* reacts immediately to psychosomatic stress. Through massage of the G-spot and other points inside the vagina, a woman can have a beautiful opening, which may start with tears of relief. The results can be blissful and can transform into tantric orgasms.

While tantric rituals are derived from ancient texts and have been known for centuries, with tantric massage, the opposite is true – it is not mentioned in the tantric tradition. Many people may be surprised to hear that, but actually the ancient tantrics did not need massage. Their bodies were already quite pure and they were practicing a lot of *Hatha Yoga*. At the time when Tantra was famous in India – and we are talking about hundreds and even thousands of years ago – there was much less stress, no pollution, food was much more natural, and there was no social shame associated with nudity and sexuality. So the early tantrics didn't have a lot of physiological and physical issues. Today we have a lot of stress in our lives and our senses are overloaded with all kinds of information. In addition, experience shows that emotional traumas in both men and women are more commonly seen nowadays. Modern tantrics realize that massage has become increasingly necessary for people living high-paced, stressful lives, who find it difficult to shift to a sexually relaxed state in order to experience Tantra with their partners. One great way to ease this transition to sexual intimacy involves the use of tantric massage.

You may do a ritual or massage, or both if you have the time. Tantric massage is a method of massaging one's partner especially with the use of energy. Of course, any skillful, authentic massage can be very helpful for purifying and removing stress from the body, allowing partners to become more open and sensual. If the massage is done more deeply to stimulate the lymph system, the lymph should move more harmoniously in the body. So, in fact, any kind of massage is beneficial.

Tantric massage itself does not have any clear origins but modern tantrics seem to have adapted their knowledge in Tantra to enhance and complement their skill in massage.

By putting them together a tantric flavor is imparted to the massage. Ayurvedic massage, which I learned from an Ayurvedic massage master, is also excellent, as it teaches how to release certain blockages in the body, especially as they pertain to the sexual energy. Freeing sexual energy and letting it flow harmoniously in the body is very beneficial for anyone on the tantric path, even more so for beginners.

Tantric massage involves the massage of the genitals. Many are very challenged by this for obvious reasons – embarrassment, guilt or shame, psychological issues connecting pleasure and deserving it with self-worth, an inability to receive touch, etc. Most people are accustomed to massage in which the genitals are completely skipped and the topic is ignored, usually because an underlying fear exists regarding improper behavior, abuse, or simply inappropriate touching. This subject is usually shameful for many people, who hide and cover up this part of the body and don't want to deal with it. However, when you do massage you need to understand that the genitals are natural and intrinsically part of our bodies.

In addition, the genitals are a very important part of the body. According to Tantra and Chinese Taoism as well, our genitals are reflexive organs, meaning that various parts of the body, and in particular the organs and glands, are connected by points within this region as described in zone therapy. For example, if a man's penis and testicles are massaged properly, not only can he learn how to overcome oversensitivity, premature ejaculation, and other men's problems, but also the organs of the body are reflexively stimulated and energized. Men can learn how to diffuse their sexual energy, spreading it throughout the body and becoming full-body orgasmic, rather than keeping it stagnant and localized in the penis. A woman who is skillful in tantric massage can help a man feel his energy and spread it throughout his body, although of course men can do this for themselves, too, to a certain degree. It is a big help for men.

For women, it is even more critical and mind-blowing because women cannot only learn to move energy, but can release tension, stress, and blockages of various kinds (especially psychosomatic) in the vagina. Tantric massage of the vagina can be an overwhelmingly transformative experience. In modern times, unfortunately, most women have some sexual blockages which are confronted through tantric massage. I have done this kind of massage for years and have seen the powerful transformation which can occur for each woman. Women often find the massage deeply releasing, exactly because they hold so much tension and suppressed emotion in that area, often due to negative experiences from the past. The massage may be intense, allowing a woman to let go of unhelpful emotions, cry, or unlock memories from the past which had held them back from happiness, pleasure, orgasm, or other things. By releasing these blockages a woman can start to peel off other layers impeding her full potential.

❧ During tantric massage, when the partner is fully and sincerely trying to help the energy move, then magic happens! I had felt many times energies moving upward and often needed to cry. I had a huge experience where I cried for a while, deeply; it came out from nowhere... The brain was empty, but tears were streaming out like crazy, and the body wanted to bend on itself, like a fetus. I could feel a deep sadness in this moment. But it's difficult to be aware of feelings or why those tears are there, stuck since a while.

Every time after a tantric massage, my sexual sessions are amazing, strong. I feel more powerful, aroused sexually, passionate. I feel more pleasure quicker and stronger. I feel energy moving clearly and upward.
— *Amandine*

I'd like to share two women's experiences with tantric massage. One woman had a lot of pain in the vagina when she made love and even when she rode a bicycle – the seat and pressure were simply too uncomfortable. After only one massage, which took only 30 to 45 minutes and was only partly a genital massage (and not even a complete one at that), she opened up and started to feel certain things. The massage unlocked some blockages for her, in her case leading to female ejaculation, which can be an enormously relieving orgasmic experience. She told me afterward that since the massage everything had changed for her. She could ride a bicycle happily, with no pain whatsoever, she now made love without pain, and she experienced much more pleasure. The pain had been locked there psychosomatically.

A second woman had been in psychotherapy for 10 years because she was sexually abused when she was young. She told me that she came to one of my workshops and she and her partner did tantric massage focusing on her G-spot. She had such a powerful experience and relief that it almost stopped her breathing – so much stuff had to come out! She told me that by the time it ended, she felt that she had made more progress toward resolving her sexual issues than she had in all her years of therapy. That is how powerful it can be, and I have witnessed this over and over. Tantric massage can be overwhelmingly great support for eliminating sexual blockages and restoring health at many levels.

Originally tantric massage was not meant for that. It was meant to provide a woman with multiple orgasms, opening her to the magical universe of tantric orgasm. But if a woman is too blocked at this level, she needs to overcome such limitations first, before attention is turned to orgasm. The area needs to be gently caressed, working out what inhibits full sensation and expression. Then slowly, in a process that's very individual and may take from two to 20 treatments, massage awakens orgasm or even a range of orgasms and lovemaking becomes an incredible, fulfilling experience.

Regarding the different points in the vaginal area, this is a study which requires more explanation than I can give here (but which we explore in detail during my workshops). However, certain points are very important to mention. One is the G-spot, which – while accepted in modern sexology – continues to be viewed with skepticism among medical professionals as an urban legend or myth that has no proof. Indeed, it is a very real spot, an area inside the vagina. Most men, regrettably, have no idea where it is, but even more sadly, many women also don't know. In Tantra, the G-spot can lead to multiple orgasms (G-spot orgasms), which are unbelievably pleasurable and long-lasting – more incredible than anything most women have ever experienced. Yet for a woman who doesn't know its location, which is the first obstacle, the G-spot is not even really relevant. Once this point is stimulated properly, still there are more obstacles. For example, some women cannot feel anything. When I massage them and ask if they can feel something, they respond that they feel nothing. But not feeling at all is not OK – it's a blockage. On the other hand, some women feel severe pain, irritation, a burning sensation, the need to urinate – many reactions can arise. Thus, G-spot stimulation needs to be approached properly. If done properly such stimulation can even trigger female ejaculation, which is a very positive experience that can help a woman open up a lot. And women do not lose energy with female ejaculation, which can eventually lead to tantric and G-spot orgasms.

The tantric massage course was a life-changing experience for me. It influenced me most positively and the effects continued long after the course. I enjoyed every second of the course; the group energy that emerged between the participants was just wonderful. For the first time in my life I experienced unconditional love between people with a common cause, willing to give and receive, learn and experience, trust and surrender completely. The course changed my life enormously in many ways. The awareness about myself and my body has increased and I am much more open and courageous. The change that the course triggered in me has been lasting and will surely continue in the future. The experience was so deep and massive, it led me to change the course of my life and step on a new path. Since the course I've had opportunities to practice tantric massage and it has made my sexual experiences more pleasurable.

During an intense massage I even experienced female ejaculation. It feels very close to the world's most wonderful orgasm!

I practice tantric massage always when there's an opportunity, for it's an ultimate pleasure and pleasant pastime that unites partners on the most intimate level. Tantric massage provides the opportunity to give and receive sublime emotions and create moments that are superior to any other intimate experience.

— *Liina*

GREAT LOVERS DON'T RACE FOR EJACULATION

For men tantric massage presents new scenarios. First of all, most men would love to become excellent lovers and yet many don't know how to go about it. Even some who want to become world-class lovers are not willing to make efforts in that direction – they want to do the minimum. However, for those who want to become better lovers and are willing to make efforts, learning how to do tantric massage will open up amazing new horizons. By learning to massage women, specifically through tantric massage, and by learning how to sublimate and focus energy in the body, these men will be on their way.

Tantric massage is not simply physical massage; it is something more like Reiki combined with massage, which means that energy moves from the giver to the recipient, plus the tissues are kneaded and energized and lymph is well circulated. The focus of the mind is essential during tantric massage. If as a man you lose focus and your energy goes to your penis, there will be a sudden and noticeable difference in the energy, which will be transmitted somehow through your hands. Men who learn tantric massage become much more tender lovers. In addition, for those with fragile egos who need to know they are good lovers, the genuine and evident pleasure the woman expresses is a good boost to the male ego.

Secondly, for a man, receiving tantric massage can help him to move his energies and learn how to control himself so that sex is no longer a one-way ticket to ejaculation. While most men are in love with ejaculatory orgasm, in reality it pales tremendously compared to what can be reached within the spectrum of male orgasmic potential. In Tantra we teach men to become multiorgasmic, a process which involves learning how to control their ejaculation. At first many men are very disappointed – they are in love with their ejaculation and don't want to give it up! Some even say it is their last pleasure in life. However, in the big picture, these men don't realize that they are holding onto the toy car of orgasm when they could trade it in for a Ferrari. They can always go back to ejaculation – this is child's play and not difficult. But if a man is willing to open his mind and learn these things, to both give and receive tantric massage, he often discovers suddenly a very amazing new energetic and sexual realm.

Hidden within our bodies are incredible energies which can be unlocked and freed by tantric massage. During one of my workshops, one man began tantrically orgasming during the massage, and he simply couldn't stop for half an hour. We had already finished the massage and he kept orgasming. We talked with each other and he was orgasming at the same time. He was shocked and laughing, and said it was incredible. It was truly a beautiful thing to witness. For guys removing blockages is not the same as it is for women. As male sexual organs are external they don't hold the same blockages as women's internal organs. We teach techniques which can remove some blockages and have amazing effects. Also in the *lingam* (penis) there are some special points which, when pressed, can release blockages.

If women do tantric massage for their partners, they need to keep in mind that it should be done in such a way that the man does not lose control and ejaculate. In my course I have noticed that there are lots of guys who guide their partner in a way that could lead them very quickly toward ejaculation. I have to remind them at that point that they need to avoid the usual jerk-off style and approach it altogether differently. Men also need to learn how to receive, let go, and surrender. You can't learn it from a book. Rather, you must sit and experience it. This requires practice with a partner and it is very highly recommended to exchange massage with a few other partners in order to feel and experience different types of energies. Some couples are afraid of opening up by including other partners in massage, but it is recommended in Tantra. It is like going to a doctor for an important surgery, and hearing the doctor say, "I am very good because I have practiced with one patient my whole life." You would probably go see another doctor because it seems like common sense that you cannot become the best and learn everything with just one person. If you allow yourself to work with a variety of partners, you will be able to give your partner a much better massage – and of course, we must remember that tantric massage does not imply or include sex, unless both partners wish for it. Otherwise, tantric massage can be done with a few partners with no actual sex but as pure therapy, sharing a heart connection and providing much needed help.

EXERCISE: AN EXAMPLE OF A SHORT VERSION OF TANTRIC MASSAGE FOR WOMEN

After bathing and making sure that you both will not be disturbed, the woman should lie down on her stomach naked, covered with a towel, sarong, or light sheet or blanket. The man will sit next to her, on her left side if he is right-handed or to the right if he is left-handed. Instructions below will be given with a presumption for right-handedness.

Put your right hand on the woman's lower back and your left hand between her shoulder blades. Feel her energy while sending her love from your heart.

Make sure to have natural oil next to you and ready for the massage. Before starting the massage, ask the woman to approve the oil and be sure that she likes its scent. However, please note that for the yoni portion of a tantric massage, a water-based lubricant should be used.

Pull the covering all the way down to her waistline, and start applying oil to the back. Gently massage the back, focusing on two lines of energy which exist parallel to the spine but about three or four centimeters away, along both sides of the spine. In tantric massage, we rely on the knowledge of energy channels and points in the body; these two lines described above are the most fundamental, because through them we can propagate the sexual energy and circulate it harmoniously throughout the body. While placing the hands fully on each side of the spine, slide the thumbs of each hand along these lines described above in an upward motion toward the head. Start at the points close to the sacrum, where two dimples are found on most people.

There are various movements and maneuvers that can be used here, but the most important thing is to remain in close contact with the skin, use ample oil so that the skin never pulls and friction is reduced, and make sure you apply a good amount of pressure.

Massage following your intuition or any training you have received and be sure to send energy from your hands to the body of the woman at all times.

Cover her back with the towel and uncover her buttocks. Now massage the gluteal muscles of the buttocks and legs while applying a decent amount of oil. Remember to use not only touch but energy, channeling passion and desire through your hands and fingers.

Now she may roll over onto her back. Hold the cover above her so that she may discreetly reposition herself on her back. Again, cover her so that she will not become chilled. Turning now to the woman's front side, start by massaging the area of the breasts, being careful not to touch the nipples in the beginning. Continue to the shoulders and down to the midsection and abdominal area. Around the abdomen be careful not to apply pressure that is too strong, unless you are sure the woman has an empty stomach. Massage the abdomen using clockwise movements. After covering up the upper torso, continue to the legs and feet, massaging with care and love and using as much oil as necessary.

At this point the woman will be very relaxed and ready for a *yoni* massage (the vaginal massage). If you did not yet learn the art of *yoni* massage, you may stop here and cover the woman up. After a break for rest, make sure to hug her and share some love and intimacy.

The practice of *yoni* massage is comprehensive and will be covered in future books. Those who have studied *yoni* massage techniques in a workshop may continue at this point to perfom such massage on their partner.

X

IMPORTANT ELEMENTS IN A TANTRIC LIFE AND A LOOK AT THE TANTRIC LIFESTYLE

The tantric lifestyle is not something you will read about in tantric texts, nor is it dictated in the way that some religions prescribe certain behavior. From my own background of being born and raised within the Jewish tradition in Israel, I've seen that the more orthodox you become in your religious approach, the more strictly it dictates almost every step of your life, without much room for spontaneity. Tantra is different. In the ancient tantric teachings we do not find any clear dogmas or models prescribed for practitioners. Rather, guidelines are presented that may be chosen according to the individual. As long as we adhere to the basic principles that are meant to protect our health and energy, we are free to follow the tantric path, choosing the various tantric options that fit each of us best.

Tantrics develop certain lifestyles naturally, as a result of their sexuality, view of the universe, and reliance on **Tantra as a spiritual teaching – a system that is meant for the evolution of human consciousness**. When a person enters the world of Tantra it will definitely manifest in his or her lifestyle – the question only remains exactly how it will manifest. My experience in tantric communities for many years has shown that tantrics usually have a certain lifestyle. They all work with energy, which means that everybody is doing *Hatha Yoga*, and many also do *pranayama* techniques, *Kundalini Yoga*, and daily meditation. This is simply what they love to do – nothing is forced or required. Not only do they develop themselves through practice, but they also avoid the stagnation that can occur without it. It is actually a normal and healthy way of living life. Naturally, many tantrics choose a vegetarian diet and strictly avoid smoking, alcohol, and drugs.

❦ Involving spirituality in life offers the ecstasy of living, the perfection of being in the moment. I've chosen Tantra as my spiritual path because Tantra considers the body as life's temple and life as the experiment of being. Tantric spirituality is something that is transpersonal; it is born between people in each moment and it is reinforced by practice. It suits me. I'm drawn to spirituality by the urge to know who I am. Through Tantra I explore my limits and expand my being.

I've used tantric practices (meditations, transfiguration, rituals) to achieve higher states of consciousness – bliss, the state of universal love and ecstasy, and the feeling of being one with the world. I have experienced all of these states through tantric practices. This gives me the feeling of opening. I experience various energies, as well as the loss of time and space. I know that all of these feelings, experiences, states of consciousness are in me, and I have experienced them in different situations and moments. Tantra enables me to induce these comparatively easily.

— *Mirjam*

AN OUNCE OF PRACTICE IS WORTH A TON OF THEORY

In Western civilization many people are very happy to read books, discuss subjects, and have an opinion. They benefit a lot from interesting theoretical conversations, and sometimes even change their way of looking at life as a result. **But the truth is that changes are the result of actual practice. The renowned yogi Swami Sivananda** once said, **"An ounce of practice is worth more than a ton of preaching."** That is absolutely true – theory is useful but it is very limited without practice. India is known for its ancient pundits – people who were scholars, teachers who mastered the four Vedic scriptures and Hindu rituals, law, religion, or music.

Some of these pundits amassed huge amounts of knowledge, remembering whole books by heart and able to debate and talk intricately about all kinds of things their whole lives – without really getting anywhere. Yogis, on the other hand, believe that theory is important, but it is completely fruitless without practice. They believe that daily practice is the only way by which a person begins to see real changes in their lives. All tantrics are daily practitioners who additionally do *tapas*. In the Yoga tradition *tapas* – translated as "austerities" or "practices of self-discipline" – is one of the *yamas* and *niyamas*, the yogic guidelines and recommendations for a healthy and harmonious lifestyle. This applies for both – yogis and tantrics.

To follow a *tapas* is to take a resolve, to make a commitment in which nothing can stop you. A *tapas* is a way of disciplining the mind and body and it only works if it is taken 100 percent seriously, because the principle of *tapas* is very simple. If your life is too soft, relaxed, and comfortable, you simply become lazy and change happens very slowly. It does not mean that you have to suffer, but it does mean that you challenge yourself regularly because a little bit of difficulty can go a long way in helping ourselves progress. As we know from the history of mankind, during times of war some of the greatest inventions were created because people, when pressed in difficult situations, tap their deepest creative intuition.

In Tantra a *tapas* is a discipline which ensures that the tantric practitioner commits seriously to his or her tantric practice and thus guarantees results. In simple words, a *tapas* is a commitment to a practice of a chosen kind (usually recommended by a teacher) for a fixed timeframe. By virtue of making a *tapas*, the resolve can never be broken, which grants enormous willpower and guarantees results in Tantra.

ASPECTS OF THE TANTRIC LIFESTYLE AND SEXUALITY

Many tantrics are aware of the tantric teachings on sexuality and choose to use this knowledge, with manner of use dependent on the personal preferences and character of the person. Some people, very situated in their practices of tantric sexuality and fully multiorgasmic, begin to experience such openness and love that they wish to share this with several partners. Others feel that they can go more deeply within a relationship with just one person. Regardless of which path one chooses – and both are perfectly valid options – tantrics are sexually openminded people.

Tantrics put a very high level of importance on the cleanliness and purity of the body and personal environment. In addition to a great level of hygiene, tantrics also adhere to sophisticated purification techniques derived mostly from the *Kriya Yoga* tradition. Originally *Kriya Yoga* was a Yoga style of purification, which fits very well with tantrics' general level of purity in their lifestyle.

ABOUT THE COSMIC RHYTHMS

Most tantrics in my lineage are aware of the teachings of astrology as they relate to Tantra. Some are amateurs with only limited basic knowledge at their disposal, but others are experts in astrology. Due to the New Age movement – which swept through many societies fostering a feel-good, watered-down spirituality which was largely based on some superficial perspectives and very big imaginations – astrology also became associated with spiritual fluff. In reality, it is an extremely elaborate, exact, and powerful so-called "occult science" from ancient times. While several branches developed in parallel in the Indian, Chinese, and Western lineages, astrology originally was a system based on the same principles as Yoga, Tantra, and all other spiritual teachings.

Astrology relies on an understanding that the universe is holographic, just as Tantra does. This means that everything in the universe is connected to everything else. We are all part of this matrix in one way or another. The forces of the universe work in a way that has been understood and defined by modern science in large part, but not entirely. A famous anecdote shows that even famous scientists have studied astrology. When the astronomer Edmond Halley (1656-1742) of comet fame once spoke depreciatively on the subject of astrology, Isaac Newton is said to have berated him with the remark: "Sir Halley, I have studied the matter [while] you have not!" In other words, don't talk about what you don't understand. Astrology is a legitimate and real domain which substantiates the influences exerted between heavenly bodies, especially the planets of our solar system. The ancients had noticed that the planets generated effects, with the gravitational shifts of these masses actually producing various forces. And those forces affect the human being. These effects are not measurable with modern tools, which is why most people think they do not exist. But they are there. Tantra understands these forces, which explains why tantrics study astrology and find a very valid system within it. As a result, they realize that different astrological moments during a month or year are very significant, and they use these auspicious moments especially for taking more important actions.

The reality is much bigger than this. There is a very esoteric and secret science from Yoga which deals with *prana*, the life force energy found throughout the universe. That science can tell you when to take any action in your life if you choose to. It will synchronize you with different forces that guarantee an action will be harmonious and successful, and it also advises what actions to avoid. This discipline can be so accurate that, for example, if you sit down for lunch and suddenly a thought comes into your head (for example, "What will happen to my sister in the hospital – will she survive or not?"), you would want to check immediately the time this thought arose in your mind. There is no such thing as coincidence and everything is connected to everything in Tantra, and accordingly, you would want to create an astrological chart for exactly that moment. If you could read such a chart properly, you would be able to see the answer to your question, whether your relative survives or not.

Most of the tantric lifestyle is connected to astrology and special moments are not necessarily astrological. For example, a big shift in energy can occur due to other reasons. A very simple example involves human conventions such as New Year's Eve. For many people, this is just a moment of celebration because the year changes. But tantrics say it is a great moment of shifting energy because, in the collective consciousness of humanity, that moment is special because everybody is aware of it, which makes it a more powerful moment. If you know what to do in this moment instead of just drinking champagne, you can actually affect the whole next year positively for both yourself and others or your country as a whole. It does not mean that you can't enjoy your New Year's Eve. For just 20 minutes before or after midnight you can do a meditation to make that critical moment an auspicious one for your future. And then continue with your celebration. It does not mean that you can't have fun – just catch the important moment.

THE UNIVERSAL ENERGIES OF DEITIES

Deities have existed in many traditions since ancient times and, according to Tantra, certain energies are universal. These forces, called cosmic powers, are related to the divine consciousness and Tantra works with them. One who studies Tantra is eventually initiated into the knowledge of cosmic powers, the *Dasha Maha Vidyas*. This is a grand teaching in Tantra, and initiated yogis begin the practice of some very advanced techniques to bring themselves into resonance with these beneficial energies. Tantrics know that this helps one's spiritual evolution, and the knowledge of these great entities is integrated into their lifestyle.

INITIATION – THE *VIRYA* POWER
IMPRINTED INTO YOUR AURA

Yoga and Tantra must always be taught from a teacher directly and never learned only from books. Books can open the gates of understanding. But the actual training must be done on a personal basis. **This process, which is called *initiation*, involves receiving a form of energy transfer and support from a teacher, in addition to the provision of a semblance of protection**, so that the student is safe, correct practice is verified, and guidance points a student toward positive results without mishaps. In the tantric tradition, as you progress in your practice and understanding, you receive successive initiations.

Since some aspects of teachings are theoretical and others are practical, just reading a book cannot represent an initiation. This is where a teacher comes in. When the teacher gives a teaching, whether theoretical or practical, it is called an initiation because that teacher has already reached satisfactory and proven results in that technique. Thus sharing the knowledge is more like imprinting it in a student's aura, rendering it more accessible to him or her. With that initiation, a student will get much better results. This applies especially with initiations in *mantras*, and with certain energies and techniques, such as those working with *kundalini*. Initiation makes a big difference; without it, the practice will suffer a lot and lack potency, will likely be incorrectly performed, and – most importantly – initiation hides within it an element of protection given by the guru and the lineage, without which the practitioner is left vulnerable to unpredictable and sometimes dangerous effects.

MILAREPA'S QUEST FOR INITIATION AND ENLIGHTENMENT

The incredible story of Milarepa, the greatest yogi of Tibet, is a classic from the history of Yoga. He started out in life as a black magician, criminal, and murderer, who later had a great transformation in life. He was taken as a disciple by guru Marpa, who realized that Milarepa had a great deal of negativity and karmic baggage. Marpa understood that Milarepa needed to burn all this negative karma before he could give him higher initiations and teachings. Because he was teaching a person who still had low energies, he had to treat Milarepa poorly in the beginning – it was a test for him.

Milarepa worked hard at various chores and tasks which were meant to test him, and he suffered. But this was the only way to help him change, to overcome his ego, to burn the negativity he had collected due to his horrible behavior in the past. Eventually, at some point Milarepa – who was a very strong character and was passing through many challenges – broke down and went to the wife of guru Marpa, who always helped him and tried to heal his wounds. He told her that he wanted to receive a teaching but Marpa had not given him teachings so far, only hard work and suffering. Marpa's wife – who still lived from the ego and wasn't yet a guru – was indeed very compassionate and decided to help Milarepa. So she wrote him a note forging the signature of guru Marpa and sending him to another guru. It was common at that time in Tibet for some gurus to have specialized teachings with certain initiations and for others to be masters of other techniques such that they would at times exchange disciples.

With the faked signature Milarepa escaped and went to the new guru. This guru put him in a room, taught him a technique and, as is the norm in Tibet, once you are put in a room the door is closed and no one disturbs you, except to bring food once a day or observe your progress from time to time. Milarepa did his practice the best he could. And there were no results. After a while the teacher came to see how Milarepa was progressing and saw there were no results. Something is wrong here, the new guru thought. It was then that he realized the signature had been forged and sent Milarepa back to guru Marpa, where he started again with hard work. The point of this story is that without the guru, even if you get the exact teaching, you will not get the initiation, you will not get the same results. **This is an energetic concept which has been validated for centuries**. You don't have to meet your guru twice a day; you can meet him, for example, only twice a year. But **this link has to be there. It is like a support system**.

The tantric lifestyle involves a daily routine that includes certain practices. This routine, which lasts normally from 10 minutes to a few hours a day, includes not only *Hatha Yoga* and practices of moving and controlling energy, but also meditation and purification techniques. Tantrics may also participate in rituals once a week or monthly. They will routinely do transfiguration practices and may take part in group practices if circumstances allow. Tantrics are aware of astrology – some more so, some less so. They have contact with their guru, in modern times even by email or phone, or a student will meet his guru once in a while to meditate together and receive some advice and support.

❀ My way of thinking has changed and I have reached an understanding that all begins with myself. If I wish that the world would change around me, I should start from myself. I see what I'll have to change to bring suitable things, situations, and people into my life.

My relationship with my daughter has acquired a new and improved quality. My circle of connections has changed a lot. I'm surrounded by people who support each other's development, who live and help.

I use the principles of a tantric lifestyle in my everyday life and I become braver and braver. I have taken a loving attitude toward the world into my workplace as well. As a result the people in my department are much more positively tuned. Our department scored the best results in a personnel feedback survey. The results were better and more stable. And the funny thing is that the others don't understand what's happening around me. They think it's unbelievable and try to find realistic or economical reasons for it.

With a tantric lifestyle every pleasant situation can produce an orgasm-like feeling if you enjoy it with all of your being like, for example, eating something exquisite, admiring nature, etc.

Tantra teaches you to feel and see yourself better, to notice things in a new light. By this also the worldview will change and that's wonderful. I can be free and natural, without worrying what others think about me.

— Kaidi

When it comes to sexuality, tantrics are aware that sexual energy is very powerful and they heed the directives of tantric sexuality. If tantric practitioners are sexually active, as most are, they would have a partner or partners with whom they make love regularly. And the effects of that tantric interaction would not be limited only to the sex life, but would expand to influence their general progress in spirituality.

On a more simplified level, in the Chinese tradition, for example, it is noted that the yin and yang benefit from the union of lovemaking. Yin needs a bit more yang and yang a bit more yin for balance. Tantrics say that the tantric sexual act in itself is a Yoga practice: energies are moving, *kundalini* is rising, and multiple orgasms take you to a deep state of ecstasy. All of that supports both one's tantric and spiritual progress.

Tantrics also observe a healthy diet in order to bring more purity into their lives. In addition they try to live a life which is harmonious, avoiding everything that involves violence, aggression, even extreme sports – basically anything that doesn't support their own focus on a harmonious lifestyle and action. Some people are obsessive about driving motorbikes, jumping out of airplanes, or doing bungee jumping. But this kind of thrill-seeking behavior shows a young soul. Look at children – they want to try anything; everything is so interesting for them. But as you grow older you realize that you don't have to try everything because you know what is important. The more spiritual you become, you understand that it's not wise to put yourself in unnecessary danger. It does not mean that you don't do fun things or that you are scared of living – tantrics love fun, dancing and singing, making love, and plenty of other exciting activities. But they still do their best to keep life harmonious, relaxed, and beneficially oriented.

KIDS AND TANTRIC FAMILIES

While most people believe that having children is almost given up to chance, Tantra regards tantric families in a very spiritual, almost metaphysical way. Tantra considers that having children can be done much more spiritually than how it normally occurs. Usually two people are in a relationship and have sexual intercourse for the sake of sex, with or without the intention to have children. If they intend to have kids, they have a romantic dinner and some wine, get in bed, have sex, and that's it. (If they don't intend to have kids it looks about the same, but may involve birth control precautions.) Soon they begin checking whether they got pregnant or not.

Tantra says far more is at stake here and the process should be much more conscious. Many tantrics believe in the concept of reincarnation, which purports that the human soul does not die at the time of physical death. That means that some aspect of ourselves which is fully us remains in existence at a subtle level and moves on to another process. The soul will reincarnate at some point, returning in the form of a child, and not actually in a short time as is depicted in some scenarios. Therefore, the tantrics say that the number one thing to understand is how to act properly as a couple in order to determine which soul will reincarnate in your child.

Remember. The way you make love
is the way God will be with you.
— Rumi

How does that work? First of all, tantrics say that the lovemaking act is important in itself. There is a theory in the Tibetan tradition which postulates that the soul is somehow attracted to a couple making love by resonance with that couple. Thus, through the law of attraction, when making love in the tantric style, certain secret teachings (which can only be given by a teacher personally with initiation) can be applied in order to create a certain frequency of energy that will attract a certain soul. For this reason, tantrics prepare consciously to have children when they do. They begin the childbearing process by taking good care of themselves, choosing an exemplary diet for the months prior to conceiving, because the body is usually a bit slow in exhibiting the improved health bestowed by a high-quality diet. It can take months before the diet affects all the tissues deeply, manifesting a cleaner and more harmonious body, at least physically.

Next the partners will meditate regularly and perform a ritual for the moment of conception. They will make love as tantric lovers and make sure they enter deep states of orgasm which bring the mind into higher and more spiritual levels of consciousness. When they allow the ejaculation to occur, the woman gets pregnant. In modern times, many couples struggle to get pregnant. It is not a surprise because research has shown that many men have either an extremely low sperm count or, due to chemicals and impurities, sperm with low motility – an inability to reach the woman's egg. Tantric men who know how to control their energy also know how to maintain powerful and healthy sexual energy, and therefore attempts at pregnancy are usually immediately successful. The man's sperm is strong and healthy, both partners control their energy well, and in most cases, pregnancy is achieved more efficiently and quickly.

From the woman's side, during her nine months of pregnancy, she does not eat whatever comes to mind. Today apparently it's acceptable to indulge any cravings as a pregnant woman, even cravings for junk food or unlimited chocolate. And everybody smiles and understands – it's because she's pregnant, what to do! Tantrics would not endorse such an unrestricted diet because the food a woman eats during pregnancy actually creates the child. If she eats junk food for nine months during her pregnancy, her diet will negatively impact the life growing inside her. The building blocks that will be used to create the baby will be of very poor quality. Women should keep a very healthy diet during this period. Some tantrics recommend a macrobiotic diet in order to balance the expectant mother's yin and yang energies. Definitely the diet should be rich and healthy, with all the nutrients she needs. A mother-to-be should do Yoga regularly so that the child will be born properly and safely, of moderate size, healthy, and harmonious. In spiritual environments, cases have been documented in which expectant mothers who kept healthy diets, meditated regularly, and practiced spiritual disciplines during pregnancy bore children who did not cry at birth but rather smiled!

Children also grow up differently in a tantric family. They will learn how to eat and behave correctly and maybe even how to meditate at a young age. I witnessed this while living within a large tantric community. One day we all did a meditation together and at some point I heard little footsteps. A small child, maybe 4 years old, came and joined our group, sat down, closed her eyes, and started meditating. She continued the meditation with everybody else until the end.

I was amazed! That was a tantric child. Tantrics really do have a unique approach to family planning and family life.

❋   In our family Tantra has increased our harmony together, and the father of the family came back to us. The gap between mother and father decreased and, finally, disappeared – the children could feel it as well. We are more tolerant, open, and free as a family than before. A tantric family changes the attitudes held toward each other; we became closer and honesty became important.
— *Ülle*

XI

TANTRIC PRINCIPLES AND TECHNIQUES

In the tantric tradition the vagina is called a *yoni*, which is a holy place – the place of life, the seal of Shakti. The penis of a man is called a *lingam*, which is also a very spiritual term denoting an organ of energy. These terms originate from ancient times and their true origin is unknown. Let's explore some of the techniques available in Tantra.

GAZING MEDITATION FOR COUPLES

It is important to reach some level of control of the mind, which for most people is chaotic, restless, and moving non-stop with thoughts. Simply asking a person to sit quietly, maintain relative stillness, detach the mind from obsessive thoughts, and become focused can be very demanding.

For these reasons, tantric meditations have a big advantage. Regular meditation requires a lot of willpower, which most people unfortunately don't have. Tantra offers meditations that deal with sexuality, and it is known that we are more attentive, keen, and aware of our surroundings when sexually aroused. Therefore, tantric meditation can be easier for modern people who are frequently exposed to sexuality and sexual content (from advertising, the media, the Internet, etc.). This meditation practice, in which the sexual energy is brought to the heart chakra while focusing in the region of the chest, can be done alone or with a partner. It is also recommended to play music that resonates with *anahata* chakra, the heart chakra, during the meditation.

If practicing in pairs, a couple should sit together in meditation bearing in mind not to become overly focused on the sexual act itself. Try to feel what you want to feel while making love with your partner. Sit facing each other either on the floor or in chairs and hold hands in any comfortable position. During tantric exercises in our classes and workshops, we teach special *mudras* – positions in which to hold hands so that energy flows through them better.

The only physical prerequisite is to sit with the spine straight and without slouching. This helps the energy flow best. If the spine is not kept in a vertical position, the effects of meditation are weakened.

Now spend a few minutes in meditation on the heart chakra, focusing the mind on that area. And then gaze into your partner's eyes, with music playing softly in the background. Spend time looking into each other's eyes for no special reason, without any expectations, just lost in these gateways to the soul. With just 10 minutes of practice, the partners will feel a transfer of energy, an opening into the other's heart, greater intimacy, and even tears.

From my experience, as funny or sad as it might sound, many partners – even those who have been together in couples for years – realize that they haven't looked into each other's eyes for a long time. Secondly, many emotions rise to the surface without even saying a word. Another reaction may be discomfort. One partner will feel agitated, have the impulse to break the gaze, or will react with excessive blinking, nervous gestures, or by otherwise creating a distraction that diverts attention from the intimacy of the moment. Usually this results from the negative reaction of the ego when the heart chakra is blocked. Sometimes such a response is the result of anger – opening yourself up when you actually don't want to. It can feel too intrusive. In Tantra this is a very clear and strong indication of a problem for which this meditation should be done regularly. If the woman has these feelings, it is likely that she also has problems with her orgasms. **In Tantra most women who cannot orgasm or are sexually unresponsive are women with a blocked heart chakra**. It is worth the extra effort to allow this connection, to peel away that which hinders the deepest layers of the heart. If emotions come, let them out – cry if you need to and for as long as necessary to release the feelings that are being cleared. To reach a harmonious and cleansed feeling, you can do this meditation for hours.

If a person laughs as a diversion during this meditation, this is another type of blockage: energy stuck at the level of the third chakra, the solar plexus, *manipura*. This person has a fear of intimacy and the ego presents the mechanism of laughter to thwart it. The ego feels superior to the practice: "This is a joke, not real, and I don't really need to do it. This whole thing will end as a humorous anecdote." Many times the next step will involve crying. Although not always the case, often once you corner the ego, the real issues come up.

THE CONCEPT OF BEAUTY

While Tantra is a spiritual path, it also has a lot of playful and humorous aspects and encompasses an appreciation of beauty. As Tantra is the worship of the feminine and the whole universe is Shakti, it definitely holds appreciation for the universe and everything in it. The great tantric masters were masters of aesthetics. Perhaps the most famous and powerful tantric master known was Abhinavagupta, who emerged from the lineage of Kashmiri Shaivists. He wrote treatises on aesthetics and harmony which are considered classics in the tantric tradition. **Tantra is the study of**

aesthetics, harmony, and beauty.

Beauty is of one of the main aspects of Tantra. It is also what everybody seeks in culture, art, music, and many other fields. As human beings we are so attracted to beauty for spiritual reasons. When we go to a museum or listen to a symphony, we are attracted to it because the beauty gives us a certain vibration, uplifting our soul and leading us to feel amazing. It actually makes us feel spiritual.

Let the beauty we love be what we do.
There are hundreds of ways to kneel and kiss the ground.
— Rumi

Today living in what has been termed the "iron age of mankind" – *Kali Yuga*, the lowest of the historical planetary cycles in Tantra – not surprisingly we find a lot of worship of and search for ugliness. Horror movies are shown at the cinema and all kinds of art are idolized that explore the low aspects of life – ugliness, weirdness, darker sides, things which can be considered the very opposite of classical beauty. People say that to be honest we need to present all aspects of life, the dark and light – that this is reality. While this is true, especially keeping in mind the duality of the mind, yin and yang, etc., we still need to remember that human beings have creative abilities and by focusing, concentrating our minds on what we want to create, we can change our reality and determine how it will manifest. Here it could be illustrative to mention the practice of tantric transfiguration we've discussed, which is a powerful way of determining which reality you wish to create for yourself. All of this works according to the principle of resonance. The more resonance with ugliness or darkness within you, the uglier your reality becomes. And of course the more you focus on purity, beauty, harmony, and light, these qualities will be reflected in the reality you manifest.

TANTRA IS FUN

And then there is also humor. Spiritual humor is amazing! Great spiritual masters were very playful and humorous, not just dry old men sitting and meditating, disconnected from the rest of the world. For example, from reading his books we may get the impression that Dr. Swami Sivananda, the great master of Yoga from India, was a very strict person, but in reality he was quite playful as well. One day while he was at his ashram in India, a band of wrestlers came to visit and present some wrestling exhibitions. They asked for volunteers from the audience to come and wrestle and surprisingly Sivananda himself was the first to step forward. He was a big guy who was physically quite overweight in his old days, but he went and wrestled with his visitors nonetheless. He was also known to pull pranks on people sometimes.

One of Sivananda's disciples was a German woman who had come to practice spirituality. She was always complaining about the spicy Indian food and how she missed the tasty German cakes from home. Then one day Sivananda came to her with a big cake. She was so happy that she cried. She took a big bite of cake and discovered that it was in actuality a fake cake made of shaving foam or something similar – and she started to cry again, this time from disappointment. Everyone had a good laugh over this episode, which had shown her still to be a slave to her emotions and desires at the expense of her spiritual progress.

When I meet with my teacher and a group of us may be sitting and preparing for a meditation, we often tell jokes to each other. I tend to remember an infinite number of jokes and so does my teacher. We can keep going all night, telling jokes nonstop until people start having stomach cramps and their faces hurt from laughing so much. Jokes and fun are important from the spiritual standpoint as well, because humor originates from *manipura* chakra, the third chakra located at the energy point near the solar plexus. This is a chakra gravely lacking in many people today, in fact quite weak all across the planet. For this reason, in spirituality we encourage people to take time for jokes and laughing. It is good to memorize some jokes to share and to be able to laugh. It's important because it actually brings the energy to the third chakra, where the fire in the body is located. It helps to move the sexual energy up and to channel it in the body. Laughing is not just for the sake of fun; it can be extremely healing.

I remember hearing about the case of a man who had cancer and his doctors said they couldn't do anything for him. He told himself that if he were going to die soon, then at least he would die laughing. So he started watching comedies, a marathon of one after another, and for days and days he did nothing but laugh. The next time he went to the doctor, he was completely healthy. He saw such results because the fire element in the body burns all impurities. *Manipura* chakra, this third chakra, is the chakra of health. So if you didn't already enjoy laughing and good humor, now you know why this is not only fun but important!

COMMON PROBLEMS WITH ATTRACTION

While rituals present an excellent method to be used as a gateway into tantric sexuality, tantric sexual technology actually involves a very simple principle: channeling of the sexual energy in the body. In Tantra, energy is always channeled upward. It also circulates in the body, following some downward movement, and at other times we direct it specifically to a certain area, like the heart. But tantrics put the most emphasis on upward movement, which can be called sublimation.

In the tantric sexual union, the lovers focus on holding back the sexual energy from the state of explosion, and directing it to their higher chakras. Most people, when they make love, simply follow the energy where it takes them – to a predominant focus in the lower chakras, especially the second chakra, the seat of the genitals. For the average person, making love leads to energetic depletion on one level or another.

Each of us has a certain amount of energy in that area when we start making love. The energy starts boiling more and more intensely and then it overflows during intercourse, accompanied by movement which normally lasts only about 10 minutes until ejaculation signals the end of the sexual liaison.

The Kinsey Reports included this data, which seems to support conventional observations:

– 17.6% of males reported ejaculation less than
  two minutes after intromission;
– 47.6% ejaculated less than five minutes into coitus;
– 22.9% claimed to have lasted 10 minutes or more.

(Table 324, p. 373: *Kinsey Data*, College Sample)

The lack of control over the ejaculation leads to a relatively quick loss of sexual magnetism and attraction between partners. In the beginning of the relationship, usually there is strong sexual desire, a lot of mutual attraction, and couples enjoy hot sex. But this is not an indicator of the long-term sustainability of sexual satisfaction and, in many cases, desire eventually fizzles out, leading many couples to seek ways to relive or reignite their passion. According to Tantra, the passion doesn't have to die. When a man learns to control his ejaculation and a woman learns to experience internal, implosive orgasms, the partners can maintain their passion and healthy sexual attraction for life.

The following suggestions include simple techniques that can be applied during lovemaking by anyone.

CONTROLLING THE SEXUAL ENERGY

Women are natural-born tantrics and, with the right sexual partner or a tantric man, they can reach multiple orgasms very quickly and perceive naturally how to control their energy. Why is this so natural for women? Physiologically, the female genitals are internal while male genitals are external. For men the fact that the energy is more external makes it much harder to control. For women, the genitals are for the most part deep inside the body and if a woman makes love with the right man, she can naturally feel and channel the orgasmic energy internally. Men tend to focus on their penis (*lingam* in Tantra). When a man makes love, in most cases, the pleasure comes from the stimulation of his genitals. Many men feel that without proper genital stimulation, the sex is not satisfying.

In Tantra we learn how to regulate the breathing and control the mind. By moving the energy up along the body to the higher chakras, lovemaking can last a very long time, with orgasm building up continuously and not characterized as explosive. It comes in waves and reaches more deeply toward what many tantrics call the "valley of orgasm." It is like surfing in the waves of orgasm without falling off the wave. You can experience orgasm as a long and deep experience, which is much more satisfying than a quick, explosive orgasm.

HOW TO ACHIEVE ALL THAT?

The first thing we would suggest is to join a Tantra workshop. In the meantime, however, it is good to remember that Tantra incorporates into its teachings *Kundalini Yoga* and *Hatha Yoga*, whose techniques can greatly move the energy upward in the body. So having a background in Yoga can lead us to use techniques for sublimation regularly that help support our tantric practice.

ABDOMINAL BREATHING!

The first practical technique for beginners is abdominal breathing. Due to our hectic lifestyles, most people tend to breathe more intensely – fast and shallow, as we do when we are excited. That means we breathe with the upper part of the body and are not able to calm down and go deeply into whatever action we do. Breathing abdominally means breathing with the lower parts of the lungs. Take deep breaths and feel the abdomen moving. This allows much better ventilation of the lungs from a physiological standpoint but it also aids in the activation of different chakras and energies.

Abdominal breathing also helps generate a certain personal power and gives much better awareness of the sexual potential. A simple exercise would be to count to seven while inhaling through the nose, and to make sure that during the inhalation you observe your body, that the belly is expanding more than the chest. For women it is a bit more difficult but they can also learn to do this relatively easily. So inhale while counting to seven, hold the breath while counting to seven, and then exhale through the mouth also while counting to seven; all the while, notice the abdominal movement during this exercise. It is helpful to practice this exercise several times daily. If you notice any discomfort, you can reduce the counts to five. This very simple and beneficial exercise will have as its main effect that you will become more aware of your sexual energy and you will start noticing that when you make love you can sense this energetic wave and control yourself better. It also has other effects such as lowering the blood pressure and removing stress.

You can also use this breathing technique while making love. Most people have sex unconsciously, with no awareness of the breath until sex is over and they collapse. With this simple breathing exercise, a wild unconscious experience can be transformed into conscious lovemaking.

While you are making love, apply your attention globally to your entire body without limiting it to any specific part. Later on, you'll learn to pay attention to your partner's body in a similar way as well. When you make love in this way you are observing your own breathing, which can be challenging because often sex is over so quickly that people say they can't pay attention to anything but trying to reach orgasm.

In Tantra lovemaking is not a race. You take your time, slow down, and pay attention to your own body. If you pay attention to your breathing, you'll notice when it becomes irregular. Then you can modulate the breathing, slowing it down and consciously taking deep breaths. In this way, you can also regulate your lovemaking and turn it into a slower and more enjoyable experience. And when you do that, you'll notice that your energy is much more under your command. You can then pay more attention to your partner and his or her body, to your own body, and just enjoy the process.

LOVEMAKING IS A HOLISTIC EXPERIENCE

Another technique is more like a way of being. This applies mostly to men but women should also pay attention to something we call the art of love – making love not for the purpose of orgasm. Men especially have been conditioned to make love as a race for orgasm. The art of love involves making love slowly, without setting in your mind the end of the lovemaking, and simply enjoying the experience itself. Touch your partner anew, with the right variety and appropriateness for the moment. Pass your fingers gently over the skin of your partner, smell your partner's body and skin, enjoy the textures, use your tongue gently, applying pressure or removing pressure – just being present for your partner and spontaneously responding in the moment is essentially the purpose of this technique.

LEARNING TO SENSE ANOTHER PERSON WITH IDENTIFICATION

The art of *samyama,* or identification with one's partner, represents another, more advanced technique in tantric lovemaking. *Samyama* involves the ability to concentrate on your partner until you can sense him or her. Once you can sense your partner, you don't need to hear their verbal requests – you simply understand and feel what he or she needs. Tantric lovers do this all the time, naturally and instinctively entering a state of identification in which they can feel their partner in a perfect synchronization. It is almost like magic. You feel and desire your partner in the sense of celebrating your intimacy and you feel the deep wish to both give and receive love. In my workshops I teach this as more of a physical initiation. The easiest way to learn this is by doing tantric massage for your partner. From there, it is very easy to take it to the level of lovemaking.

Wherever you are, and whatever you do, be in love.
— Rumi

GIVING IS RECEIVING

Another technique is called the principle of pleasure, which involves opening the heart chakra. In this approach, instead of focusing on your own pleasure, you focus fully on the pleasure of your partner. If you make love with this in your mind, leaving your ego behind, feeling that you are giving everything you have to your partner, remarkably, people reach incredible orgasms with this approach. **Those who give get incredible orgasms**. The principle at work here is that, because you open your heart chakra and really focus on giving pleasure, you have opened the gate through which not only everything can be given from you but also everything can come in. I have seen this phenomenon play out many times. A woman makes love, trying to attain orgasm, but she can't. The next second she thinks, I just want to give him all the pleasure. And suddenly she reaches orgasm.

LONG FOREPLAY IS ESSENTIAL!

Foreplay is very important, especially for women. Most of the time when a man gets an erection he thinks the need for foreplay is over – next up is penetration, then orgasm…. For women it does not work this way. A man needs to approach lovemaking in such a way that he does not think about sex *per se* but that he is there to give his woman a lot of pleasure – his gift for her today.

Sometimes even just hugging a woman, whispering something into her ear, and breathing on her neck can represent 50 percent of what she needs in the way of foreplay. Sometimes even making her laugh is enough to get her halfway ready to make love. Laughter can make women very easily sexually open – already a good beginning.

The next step in foreplay is touching her in the right way, doing some massage, continuing to be a bit playful. And it is important not to be stressed out about all this. If you can relax and enjoy at first just the massage it is already a step forward to lovemaking. It is always recommended not to start with the erogenous zones – buttocks, breasts, and genitals. Start slowly with the belly or neck, watch her breathing, give her a head massage…. Just enjoy the whole process and you will see when the woman is ready.

> *With the first two fingers, touch the partner's head,*
> *forehead, eyes, throat, earlobes, breasts, upper arms,*
> *heart, navel, thighs, feet, and sexual organ. Charge*
> *these places with the vital energy of transformation.*
> — *Yogini Tantra*

Featured in one of its old texts, Chinese Taoism has a scale for understanding a woman's sexual excitement. There we find mention of nine stages that indicate the signs of a woman's arousal. The signs are, for example: the breath becomes heavy and saliva is produced, the body and muscles become soft, the blood heats up and the woman reaches to touch her partner everywhere, etc. The point is that we do that all subconsciously anyway. We all have a talent for reading our partner's body language, but we do it subconsciously and without even noticing. However, if we do this while lovemaking, really observing and perceiving our partners, we can very easily interpret their reactions and know what to do.

Not everyone is a good kisser, it goes without saying. Kissing is not just putting the lips together! Kissing is an art which was studied in Tantra and Chinese Taoism. The mouth is a very special organ by which we can absorb a lot of *prana* or energy. We can also exchange energy with the tongue. Learning how to kiss correctly can transform kissing from ho-hum to amazing.

Here are a couple of simple and helpful kissing techniques. A kiss should be a combination of sometimes strong but mostly soft caressing with the lips, with the mouth in a relaxed state. Don't use your tongue in the beginning. Start by simply relaxing the mouth and cheek muscles. Kiss in a soft way, just gently touching the lips to your partner's. Kiss around the mouth and neck. When your partner responds with more warmth and enthusiasm, slowly open the mouth during kissing. The tongue can be applied in gentle flickers and licks in the beginning. And when the kiss becomes more passionate, the tongue can follow suit, more active and forceful. Tongues like to interact with each other at this stage in a sexy dance. The partners may trade saliva at this point, which can create an exchange of yin and yang energy between them. Sometimes the kiss can be an orgasmic and very erotic experience all by itself.

Couples who have forgotten the art of kissing in their relationship and want to bring it back should start by doing some massage for each other. When gently touching and massaging the partner, you can start by applying your mouth, touching your partner with your mouth and lips and blowing along your partner's neck and back. This already creates the contact which will manifest the couple's erotic experience. And from there slowly work your way up. As the intensity of the intimacy and energy increases, you can kiss more and more with your mouths and tongues.

Finally, a tip – don't attack your partner! Start slowly and give your partner time to breathe. Observe your partner and when she is ready then you can add intensity. Don't expect the most passionate kissing in your first session after a long break. You will slowly build it up.

Kissing is extremely healthy as well. Research shows that those who kiss regularly – especially French-style kissing (using the tongue) – have fewer cavities in their teeth due to the balancing effect of exchanging various chemicals and hormones via the saliva. Kissing also balances yin and yang and is recommended.

A FEW NOTES ON ORAL SEX

After kissing, we turn to oral sex. In Tantra it can be done very skillfully. Tantra has devoted a lot of knowledge to the art of oral sex and its masterful techniques. One such special technique, "licking the mango," leads to a partner riding on the edge of ecstasy for a long time without losing control. This is a real, high-level art form. It's a commonly held idea that being able to make your partner explode quickly means you are a good lover. But actually the opposite is true. The real art of love is to be able to make love for a long time, to build and enhance pleasure while delaying an explosive orgasm, keeping yourself and your partner at a deeply satisfying orgasmic level, on the edge of ecstasy for a long time with no loss of energy whatsoever.

THE IMPORTANCE OF TONING AND STRENGTHENING THE SEXUAL MUSCLES

Masters of Indian Tantra and Chinese Taoism view the human body as a holistic energy system. In some texts from India the body is called "the city of nine gates," because the tantrics considered that the openings in the human body – like the eyes, mouth, ears, and of course genitals – are like gates through which we can receive or lose energy.

The upper and lower gates should be kept closed, so the life energies do not leave the body. By concentrating the ecstatic forces within, wonderful visions dawn in the mind-sky. This is a special secret, which shortens the journey of Liberation.
— Yogini Tantra

In understanding these mechanisms of the body's energy structure, they considered that we lose energy through these gates in certain ways. For example, talking too much creates a waste of energy, which is why silence is a very important practice in some spiritual traditions. But the biggest loss of energy takes place through the genitals and anus, as if the life force were leaking out.

We can strengthen and tone the muscles in the area of the perineum generally by using certain techniques. These greatly enhance the health of the body and amplify vitality, which has special relevance for the sexuality. The sexual muscles in particular not only stop energy from leaking out but the tantric tradition says that, by learning how to control these muscles, you can also control the flow of energy. If you can avoid energy loss through these gates, energy is able to circulate throughout the body, which is a key factor contributing to success in Tantra.

Sexual exercises were developed in Eastern cultures and spiritual environments that highly valued sexuality not just as a form of relaxation or pleasure but as a way of achieving harmony in life and between partners. Because of that they placed much less emphasis on the genital orgasm. In modern times people think this is the only way to orgasm. But those ancient cultures held that the human being should become focused toward whole body orgasm and holistic experiences. The orgasm must be circulated in the body, which creates transformation and brings beautiful effects physically, emotionally, and etherically. These Taoist and tantric masters considered thus that the development of the sexual muscles was the primary means of achieving, prolonging, and controlling the pleasure for both men and women.

In the West, similar exercises are also fairly well known, especially those popularized by gynecologist Arnold Kegel. His "Kegel exercises" involve contractions of the pelvic floor muscles. These were first prescribed as a remedy for problems with urinary continence and female genital weakness during preparation for childbirth. They later also become known as a method for exercising the "sex muscles." In the tantric tradition such techniques are taken to a totally new level resembling a science. Through these techniques, which control the different muscles in that area, we can control the energy movement in the body.

Such exercises for development of the sexual muscles are very important in the sexual practice of Tantra because they help control both the flow of sexual energy and the orgasm, leading to multiorgasmic states and superior lovemaking. Practitioners obtain other benefits as well, including greater familiarity with one's own genitals and sexual feelings, enhanced blood flow in the pelvic area, and improved ability to control orgasm. These exercises are also very helpful in the case of problems such as sexual unresponsiveness. Women learn how to feel more pleasure in the deeper parts of the *yoni* and sensation is strengthened. The intensity in perception increases, with women beginning to feel every little movement of the *lingam* during lovemaking. These exercises also help reduce blood flow during the period, making it much less painful and mitigating or ending PMS syndrome.

HOW TO EXERCISE THE SEXUAL MUSCLES

The first step is to find the *pubococcygeus* or PC muscles, which stretch like a hammock between the legs from the genitals to the area of the anus and tailbone – basically, covering most of the pelvic floor. The easiest way to find the PC muscles is to pay attention while you urinate. During urination, while on the toilet, stop the flow of urination on purpose, then let it resume, before stopping it again, and then relaxing. These contractions will help you recognize these muscles. For women, it is important to keep the legs more widely apart while doing this exercise so that the muscles of the buttocks don't interfere, as those muscles will also be squeezed and can send confusing signals about the location of the PC muscles.

Another exercise involves tightening the anal sphincter muscles. The best manner in which to practice this one is to take a finger, lubricate it, insert it gently into the anus, and squeeze. Try to feel the squeeze in your finger.

One way to exercise the vaginal muscles involves a woman inserting a finger into her *yoni* and squeezing. The *yoni* will hold the finger or may even push it out. This exercise can also be done with *yoni* eggs – gemstone materials, such as jade, jadeite, or rose quartz, carved into egg-shaped stones. A woman inserts the egg into the *yoni* and simply squeezes it. In the beginning you should sit or lie down to insert the egg into the *yoni* and then squeeze the muscles again and again at varying paces – quickly or more slowly. Keep squeezing at least 15 minutes, which can be quite intense. Upon completing this exercise a woman might feel a bit of discomfort in the area, because like any untoned muscle, exercise can in the beginning produce soreness. If you do this practice regularly, the muscle will become stronger and stronger, producing very good effects when it comes to sex.

Once a woman begins to notice and feel these muscles more clearly, she can do the exercises at any moment without an egg. This Kegel-style exercise of squeezing can be done while doing everyday things like housecleaning or riding the bus or can be added when making love, which greatly enhances the intensity and pleasure for a man. A woman may notice that when she tightens those muscles, her stomach or buttock muscles may also tighten a bit. This is very normal because initially it is not easy to differentiate these muscles. After some practice you can isolate the right kind of muscles easily and work with them.

The next step is to alternate short and long squeezes. Begin by contracting the *yoni* muscles 25, 30, or even more times, squeezing in rapid succession. Eventually work up to squeezing 100 times (as a set) once, twice, or three times a day. Long squeezes are simpler – you just squeeze and hold the contraction and start counting while you hold the contraction. In the beginning you can start by holding to a count of three and then letting go. You may begin with 30 squeezes and eventually build up to half an hour of practice. Of course, be careful in the beginning when the area is not yet well toned and may become sore. In a short time, the area will also start becoming stronger, leading to better results and other effects. Relax between squeezes.

A man can also squeeze the muscles to build up tone in this area. But a more advanced technique involves putting himself in erection and then squeezing the muscles, observing how the lingam moves, and counting during contractions. It is like doing pull-ups with your penis. To add an additional challenge, he can hang a small, damp towel over his erect lingam for extra weight.

The next step involves using the power of the imagination. According to the Yoga tradition the mind, energy, and body are connected. Thus, when you work on one, you can affect the others. Using the power of the mind to strengthen the PC muscles can be very helpful. For example, women can see the *yoni* as a tunnel with all of its intricate musculature and then visualize how they can contract and relax it. Men can imagine that their PC muscle is like a still cable running between their legs which they can tighten or loosen at will. These are very simple visualizations. You can even visualize light in the area of a woman's *yoni* or man's PC muscles which becomes more intense when squeezing and softens when relaxing. This helps because the mind gives a signal to the brain. Later on, because you created this link in the brain, you only have to visualize the light and it automatically gives the signal to the brain to tighten the muscles.

It is recommended to combine these techniques with Yoga techniques that circulate and sublimate the energy because these exercises may build up a lot of sexual energy in the area of the second chakra which can generate irritation or sexual hunger leading to sexual agitation. So in parallel with PC squeezes, do some techniques from Yoga which channel the energy and move it to the higher levels of the body.

While you do these exercises, give yourself positive affirmations. Every time you contract you can say a sentence in your mind like, "My PC muscles are getting stronger and stronger," or "My *yoni* is beautiful and harmonious." It gives additional energy to the muscles.

THE BENEFITS OF BREAST MASSAGE

Breast massage done properly can be very beneficial for women, affecting their hormones and lymph system in positive ways. Sometimes breast massage can help drain small lumps or cysts found during a monthly breast self-examination. According to Tantra, all lumps and breast cancer are caused by blocked sexual energy. Tantric masters recommend the use of oil for breast massage, in particular wheat germ oil, avocado oil, high-quality coconut oil, and jojoba oil.

There are various ways to massage the breasts. First of all, find a quiet place in the house and approach the massage with love and your full attention, undisturbed and fully present. To start, you can simply work from the outside in, going around the breast in a circular motion covering all sides. You can also massage from the outer areas toward the nipple, and then from the nipple back to the outer parts. Don't forget to massage the area under the armpit. Once this is done the next step is massage with a simultaneous circular motion for both breasts, moving both hands either in opposite directions or counterclockwise – the yang direction considered very useful in macrobiotics. Today most people have excessive yin energy so it is helpful to balance this with the inclusion of more yang energy.

If a woman wants to increase the size of her breasts, then introducing yang energy and wheat germ oil are very useful during massage. If it is done correctly, maybe even twice per day, and combined with tantric lovemaking, the results usually come relatively quickly. If she asks her tantric partner to help move orgasmic energy to the area of her breasts then the growth can happen even faster. To see results, you would want to do this massage approximately 10 to 15 minutes a day.

XII

TANTRA AND SPIRITUALITY

In my workshops I explain that Tantra is commonly and mistakenly regarded as some naughty, exotic, or weird sex techniques that spice up a boring sex life. But this couldn't be further from the truth. In fact, Tantra is a compendium of knowledge resembling a science. If you look at the definition, science not only reviews but also tests facts and the axioms which will become the rules to which everyone subscribes. Tantra fits very well with this. Indeed, Tantra and Yoga are often described as science experiments in which you are the scientist, the subject, and the experiment itself all in one.

These days you can see that some people are more open-minded to alternative teachings, while others consider such paths unbeneficial and laden with confusion. In other words, some people will find that an average lifestyle with a steady job, family life, and other mainstream conventions is the way to go and will consider those who are less traditional and maybe even on the "hippy" side to be lost souls. More unconventional people will tend to explore alternative festivals, a community lifestyle, shamanism, New Age pastimes, Reiki healing, and various other atypical interests. Usually more materialistic and mainstream people will consider Tantra and Yoga to be classified among such alternative pursuits in life.

Coming from a very materialistic background myself, I am fully aware of all the mistaken opinions and viewpoints about Tantra. I was a lawyer and, as all Israeli men, I also spent three years in service with the army, which was a very down-to-earth and realistic environment.

I used to do martial arts, then studied hypnotherapy and psychotherapy. So I have quite a materialistic background. When I found Tantra and began to study it, I realized that it was a very practical and powerful science. **I dare say it is the most global science you can find because it touches everything**.

I fully embrace Tantra as a teaching because it is so urgently needed in this world today. Therefore, it is not at all something to be misunderstood as one of those "alternative knowledge trends" of which there are many going around – fairy, unicorn, and confused angel workshops, and similar far-fetched interests. I am not saying these things don't have a place – many people really enjoy doing things which are very imaginative. It gives some kind of satisfaction and is fun. I accept that, but to put Tantra in the same category is a mistake.

WHAT IS THE ESSENCE OF TANTRA?

The origins of Tantra are hidden in the mists of history, not fully clear simply because they are so ancient. Some tantric texts are hundreds of years old, while others were written thousands of years ago. In written human history we cannot find information older than probably 6,000 years old, maybe some hieroglyphs or Babylonian and Sumerian records. But we are still referring to a very limited amount of knowledge from those eras, with some of it not yet properly decoded even today.

Tantra comes from very ancient times. The early tantric texts, the *agamas*, were written in the Sanskrit language, one of the planet's oldest recorded languages dating in versions to 1500 BCE. The language is very special, now written in *devanagari*, which means the language of the gods or divine language. Even as a language it was considered to have come to human beings from a divine source; I mention this because the language itself has spiritual connotations. One advanced form of Tantra – in particular the branch from Kashmir in India which is called Kashmiri Shaivism – is the crown jewel of all the spiritual knowledge of this planet. It is so advanced that for most people it either remains completely unknown or too philosophical and they don't understand how to put it into practical use.

In Kashmiri Shaivism, one of the five paths of enlightenment in the Vedic tradition of India was surprisingly the grammar of Sanskrit. Today we think that language is just a form of communication. But the ancient tantrics considered that speech – the fact that humans have articulated language and can express their thoughts and ideas in words – is a divine quality. Animals can communicate with each other, of course, but no animal has articulated language. Human beings have articulated language by virtue of their self-awareness, consciousness, and connection with the divine, which is defined in the tantric tradition as the crown chakra of the human being, called *sahasrara* in Sanskrit.

Kashmiri Shaivists studied the Sanskrit language and found it to be a form of the emanation of the universe. The universe's creation is described within the Sanskrit language because there are 50 letters (49 plus one) in the Sanskrit alphabet. The number 49 is extremely significant, because ancient tradition teaches us that the universe has seven levels of vibration and 49 is seven multiplied by seven. It appears there is only one other language in the history of humanity which is also considered divine: the ancient Hebrew language. This language has 21 (plus one) letters, which is three multiplied by seven. Again the divine number seven is represented there. So the Kashmiri Shaivists say that the study of language (and indeed the way letters are pronounced) is in itself a spiritual practice.

This gives us a bit of an indication as to **what Tantra is: a study of the universe and reality**. The tantric teachings and Sanskrit texts present a compendium of knowledge which includes vast amounts of information in many fields. Sex is one part of it, and actually quite a small part. Sex is more or less only 5 to 10 percent of all the tantric knowledge, which surprises a lot of people. Because again we return to the concept of an uninformed and confused New Age environment, and Tantra is there almost automatically associated with "that Oriental sex." People leave it at that without realizing that their understanding misses out on a huge system incorporating the study of reality and what Tantra shows us – that everything is energy.

There are various manifestations of energy and different frequencies of energy but this does not change the fact that every single thing in reality is energy. Why is that important? First of all, I would direct the reader's attention to the fact that, in the modern science of the last 100 years or so, quantum physics has also reached the same conclusions, summing up that everything is energy down to the level of atoms and electrons. This is incredible to consider because we are all made of electrons and atoms, which means that we ourselves are energy and matter at the same time. And our very reality is energy.

At this point, most people often kick back and say that this is just philosophy that doesn't really matter in their day-to-day lives. However, Tantra is extremely practical if we give it a chance. Tantrics don't believe in philosophy for the sake of mental stimulation; they believe that study is meant to lead to the practical application of knowledge. Tantrics are not magicians or illusionists. We are talking about people who literally broke the barrier between the mind of the human being and the understanding that reality is energy and are able to work with energy using only their knowledge.

Tantrics are able to use energy practically, which led many to realize paranormal abilities. Throughout history, they were able to bend space and time, and do other amazing things – that's how far it goes! The tantric texts talk about many wide-ranging and apparently unrelated subjects – from astrology and astronomy to architecture, grammar, dance, and others. Why would Tantra bother to deal with so many different subjects? Because Tantra says the whole universe is energy, and if we want to understand energy we need to understand all of its manifestations. **The more you understand energy the more you realize that every aspect of reality is just energy said in another way**.

If we understand as many aspects as possible about energy, we become more and more familiar with it. Why is that important? It's important because the whole universe is considered energy or – as tantrics define this concept – Shakti (the Goddess, power). If we understand that everything is Shakti, then the question becomes, is there anything beyond that? This is where spirituality comes in.

Tantrics say there is something beyond all the energy, known to us as manifestation or, in *Sankhiya* – the philosophy of India – as *prakriti*. There is something beyond manifestation, referred to in Tantra as the unmanifested aspect of the universe or *purusha* as it is known in the *Sankhiya* philosophy. We find the same concept in the Zen and Taoist traditions and other Eastern philosophies, presented using different terminology. Many Zen sayings, or koans, are very confusing to the logical mind. These are meant to take the mind into a realm of understanding beyond rational thinking – the realm of consciousness.

Zen practitioners have a saying: What is the value of an empty pot? Its value is its emptiness. The nothingness it contains is useful. When it is completely full, it is no longer useful in the same way for us. It can be difficult for longer useful in the same way for us. It can be difficult for the mind to understand such concepts because the mind is very much rooted in matter and experiential reality. To understand something outside this reality can be challenging. Thus, the tantrics consider there is something unmanifested in parallel with manifested reality.

SHIVA – THE UNMANIFESTED ASPECT OF EVERYTHING

This unmanifested part is the most important part. It is the part that some religions try to define with the various names of God, a higher divinity which is everywhere and watching over us. For those who cannot go further, there is an image of a wise man sitting in the clouds which helps them understand. According to Tantra, this unmanifested part is also something personified, just like Shakti – the energy personified as the Goddess. The unmanifested part is personified as Shiva, creating the "duality" of Shiva and Shakti. In truth, they are one and the same, two sides of a coin, the two complements of the whole. But this duality of Shiva and Shakti arises from the metaphysical aspects of Tantra, the philosophical play between the manifested and unmanifested. Just as the electron can be both energy and matter, reality has both aspects: unmanifested and manifested.

How is this knowledge practical for us? Reality as we know it is energy which emerged from the unmanifested realm. Somehow there was an emanation, just like the theory of the big bang in astronomy, which says the universe is continuously expanding. While this basic cosmological model of astrophysics cannot answer the question of exactly how the universe came into being, observations seem to confirm what researchers have posited: that a colossal explosion must have created the universe. But what actually exploded? What was previously there? Was it the universe in an essence-state? Was it a zero point or void?

In the same way, Tantra says that all creation springs forth from Shiva. In other words Shiva creates the universe by virtue of the power of Shakti, without which there is no power and Shiva remains a concept without manifestation. Therefore, when Shakti comes from Shiva – Shakti is Shiva. And Shiva is Shakti. And if we take this to a religious understanding it means that **God and the creation are the same**, which is a very different way of looking at things compared to the standpoints of standard religious and spiritual teachings.

Shiva is Pure Existence, the immortal Divine Principle. Shiva is Pure Consciousness, Unconditioned and Transcendental. Shiva is the deity of the Mind, the Lord of Yoga, Master of the Three Worlds, and the Conqueror of death. The whole universe is created by the Shakti of Shiva.
— Shiva Purana

Most spiritual teachings tell us that there is a God, which is beyond and divine, who watches over this reality in which we err as humans (in other words, sin) and in the end we need to aspire to reach heaven, where we will be safe in the hands of God. The problem with this way of thinking is that it views reality as a trap we need to leave behind by developing good qualities and becoming more spiritual. Tantra presents an opposite view: If Shakti comes from Shiva, the manifested and unmanifested realms are actually the same. Whatever is holy and divine created this reality, and that which is divine cannot create something which is not divine. Therefore, this reality is as divine and sacred as the One which created it. This is a different approach to reality.

Tantra sees the universe as a holy and divine environment in which everything has value. Tantrics worship the feminine (Shakti, the Goddess) because it is the same as understanding Shiva – Shiva is Shakti and Shakti is Shiva – but simply manifestation is much closer to us because we are part of it. We are living beings in manifestation. Therefore, the tantrics, being wise, realized that the practice of spirituality with the Shiva consciousness – be it a very sublime spiritual path – is more accessible for the average person by pursuing first the Shakti principle.

> *A woman initiates through that same yoni from which, in a previous life, the man was born before. A woman initiates through those same breasts which, in a previous life, suckled the man before. A woman initiates with that same mouth which once gently calmed the man before. A woman is the supreme initiatress of Tantra.*
> — *Kaularahasya*

Can you go from the physical to beyond the physical? It can take a lifetime of practice. Tantra is unique in that it studies all forms of energy. It is not mere intellectual exercise or academic study of the sciences but much more than that. It is like studying God in a way – and God is everywhere and everything. By understanding this, Tantra worships Shakti as the Goddess, which includes all of Her manifestations.

Tantra is very rich, including various teachings, meditations, visualizations, and rituals. Almost anything you can think of can be used to develop spiritually and is applied in Tantra. **Tantra sees spirit in everything.** That is somewhat close to shamanism, except that shamanism looks at things in a more simplified way in which forests have spirits or fairies, etc. While Tantra considers that everything has a spirit, it is all encompassed by an umbrella of divine spirit rather than elemental spirits or those of entities – not merely elves or fairies related to various forces. Tantra has a much more mature way of looking at embodied spirit. It is a vertical, metaphysically based, and more spiritual path compared to shamanism, which can be deemed more horizontal and earthy, practically oriented in a simpler way than the practicality of Tantra.

What is the concept of spirituality? It comes from the word spirit, obviously, but what is spirit? It is defined as the opposite of matter. Yet to be spiritual is to see spirit everywhere – the very definition of Tantra as we just explained it.

WHAT'S THE PRACTICAL USE OF THIS KNOWLEDGE?

We still need to take this understanding further toward its practical applications, as it all sounds very much like a form of theoretical science. By defining everything as spirit, Tantra considers that if we have the right attitude toward Shakti and understand what it means to worship Shakti – and this is not idol worship, a lower form of practice – we develop not only sensations, but certain spiritual or higher attitudes toward our lives and environment. These attitudes are defined by something that comes from the heart and mind.

Developing these aspects can make a person more spiritual, and thus, Tantra is a spiritual science. **Tantra defines the human being as part of the energy matrix of the universe**. And the human being is unique because it represents the pinnacle of the creation of the universe, a miniature copy of the universe. In the tantric tradition it is called the law of correspondence. If the human being is a copy of the universe, then he or she is divine. Funny enough, in the Bible you can also find there the statement that "God created man in his own image." So religions agree on this, but only Tantra puts it into terms which are useful.

Tantra claims the human being is a copy of the universe, a microcosm. Therefore, as the universe – the Macrocosm – has seven levels of vibration, so too humans have seven levels of vibration. The connection is defined and supported by the law of resonance, sometimes referred to as the law of attraction. This relationship between them is the one Tantra cultivates. Tantra guides the human being to skillfully interact with the universe via the system of chakras within each human being. The chakras are like gateways for interacting with the universe through methods drawn from Tantra, *Hatha Yoga, Kundalini Yoga, Kriya Yoga*, and various other channels including sexuality, by which the human being can open himself up more, develop, and become more and more aware of this interaction with the universe. Because we are not separated from this universe, we are fully integrated into it. If we perceive separation, it is an illusion.

❀ Tantra is amazing. I have stopped my old lifestyle (job...) and starting practicing and teaching Yoga regularly, as a lifestyle and mission. Now, I have the feeling that I'm following a path with sensibility and no longer have a blindfolded life with a feeling of loss of something important. Tantra brings light to every step, with a daily (small or big) lesson to understand, to grow and surrender.

I'm happy with this path because my life is changing for the good. I'm like an onion that Tantra is peeling every day, until reaching the center, the essential. But what can you imagine is in the center of an onion – a void? ...

Each time I practice Tantra brings me closer to the Divine.

— *Amandine*

Therefore, Tantra is a spiritual system which gives the human being greater development of the chakras, awareness, energies, and our emotions. Properly speaking, Tantra goes fully hand-in-hand with Yoga practice. Yoga and Tantra are almost synonymous; most tantrics are yogis and many yogis are somewhat tantric at least in their understanding of energy, if not in practice sexually.

TANTRA IS A SYSTEM FOR THE EVOLUTION OF CONSCIOUSNESS

When their consciousness expands, human beings understand this to be their true identity and nature. It is important to recognize that this is not an intellectual understanding because many people, especially academic types, would love to understand things intellectually and declare their understanding simply after reading some books. But this does not mean anything. I can write a book about how chocolate tastes but if you read that book you will not understand its taste – until you actually put the chocolate in your mouth and taste it. Until then your understanding is very limited and mental in scope, but nothing compared with real feelings or experience. No book can ever define experience to the point of knowing for those who haven't experienced.

True knowledge comes from an existential and experiential understanding which means actually becoming the subject. Tantra does exactly this, taking a human being and molding the consciousness there. This is the definition of evolution, which is normally very metaphysical but made practical in Tantra. Different methods of Tantra employ step-by-step techniques to reach this expansion of consciousness until a person becomes self-realized, reaching superconsciousness or enlightenment. Many different names describe the same process. You can call it liberation, *nirvana*, or *satori* as it is known in Zen. But ultimately we are talking about the same thing – the human being reaching a level of cosmic consciousness.

Once you reach cosmic consciousness, there is nowhere else to go. It is like the void explained in Buddhism, in which you focus on nothing. Nothingness means no action anymore, no movement, because we are everything. This vision of spiritual accomplishment has its downside because it promotes an avoidance of reality in the name of pursuing an ideal of the truth. This translates to asceticism, abstinence, and denial of anything that can distract us from this ideal.

Tantric spirituality, on the other hand, presents a different vision because it considers manifestation to be identical to the unmanifested realm – hence, both are as divine. This spiritual vision includes energy, matter, and everything else that makes up our reality, and therefore it embraces manifestation and does not leave it behind. It accepts the world and reality – everything reality represents, even its negative aspects – because it is all some form of Shakti, **the game of the Goddess**. We just need to understand it and then we can surpass it. It is like Shakti is playing with you. With skillfulness, you learn to harmoniously interact with Shakti. It is a beautiful play of the divine, according to the yogis of Tantra.

WHAT PART DOES SEXUALITY PLAY IN ALL OF THIS?

Tantrics consider that sexuality is based on energy. And everything is energy – specific vibrations and types of energy, including the sexual energy. In particular, the sexual energy is a very potent form of energy because it is the only form that can create life. We all come from sex. **Sexual energy is magic – it makes miracles**. It is like God blows life into reality. Tantric sexuality is based in the belief that if a man and woman connect sexually in a tantric way, the sexual interaction is transformed into a higher and more spiritual accomplishment. At the same time, that sexual connection is much more pleasurable, orgasmic, and fun.

Many people erroneously think that tantrics take sex and turn it into a boring religious experience. But nearly the opposite is true; Tantra takes sex to a whole new level of fun. The truth is that in reality average sex may be boring, which explains why so many couples complain about their ho-hum and routine sex lives. Tantric sexuality is a play of energy, where every breath, touch, and movement of energy is incredible and orgasmic.

Everyone dreams of magical, fulfilling sex that is endlessly blissful, giving multiple orgasms even into our older years. Tantra is the complete package that answers to this dream. The union of male and female, Shiva and Shakti, takes place inside us, bringing us to oneness, divinity, and spiritual fulfillment. Tantric sex can even take a tantric couple who have practiced for years to a state of enlightenment, into cosmic orgasm and ecstasy. They can reach together the same ideal that Buddhists and Zen practitioners reach, but with much more fun. That journey is a great celebration of life and happiness.

KUNDALINI TEACHINGS ARE PART OF TANTRA

A technical understanding of kundalini is quite apparent in the tantric tradition. *Kundalini* is the cosmic potential or energy, which remains a latent potential in most people. When it "wakes up" from latency, it moves into a human being's energy channels, climbing higher and higher until reaching the highest level, where it brings high states of consciousness and liberation. Some teachings in Yoga are intended specifically to awaken the *kundalini* potential.

The kundalini, blazing up at the navel center, burns up
all psychic obstacles; the ego melts and becomes transformed.
— *Chandamaharosana Tantra*

In Tantra *kundalini* can also be aroused through the sexuality. When tantric sexuality is developed properly and harmoniously, it may begin to generate a spontaneous rising of *kundalini* which is very healthy and pleasurable, representing a practice of *Kundalini Yoga* without the need to practice Yoga itself. But this requires more dedication in Tantra and is not that common. For the average person, the *kundalini* aspect of Tantra can be developed but is mild and depends on many factors such as how much time you spend on your practice, how serious your commitment to Tantra is, and so on.

Kundalini practice is considered quite secret and is kept this way with good reason. In a person who is impure or uninformed or who hasn't prepared the body fully for this powerful energetic awakening, moving the *kundalini* under such conditions can result in negative effects instead of benefits, manifesting problems for that person. The best thing to do is to find a good teacher and practice until the body is ready.

HOW TO FIND THE RIGHT GUIDE

In all tantric communities you will usually find a guru. The word "guru" can put off some people because the term has been abused in the media. It has been used to describe cult leaders who brainwash people, religious leaders who abuse their followers, etc. So in modern times the word has been misused and misunderstood. However, from the ancient knowledge of the tantric tradition, a guru is a very important and sacred concept. **The word "guru" means the one who brings you from darkness to light. In other**

words a guru, often a highly realized being, is actually a teacher.

Indians usually have a few gurus during their lifetime. The one who teaches you language is a guru, even your parents are gurus, and there are spiritual gurus if you head down the spiritual path. In the texts of Yoga and Tantra, there is a saying that without the guidance of one who has reached full enlightenment, attained true self-realization, and overcome his ego, it is very difficult to achieve results in the tantric path. Because if the person leading you is not spiritually realized, it automatically means he is still subject to the ego. And therefore, since the ego is impossible to overcome without the assistance of a guide, a guru is essential.

By contrast to Asia, where people are more innocent and sincere in this regard, in the West it's shocking to see how many people so intensely claim to have surpassed their egos, that they are fit to be gurus. When you have had the experience of meeting and knowing a detached spiritual person then you are just amazed by what you see. That is why this is quite a tricky subject. A real guru has surpassed his ego and reached high states that are confirmed. At that level, you can trust the guru, because he does not have a need to live from his ego or take actions to satisfy the ego.

The best advice for finding your tantric guide is to observe the famous saying, "The tree is known by its fruits." This tells us to avoid focusing on the external, becoming impressed by big, empty statements or superficial behavior. Be patient and observe. Listen to your intuition and inner voice. Notice the results, or fruits, of the path of the teacher himself. If you find a teacher who seems to have a lot of problems or is not in tune with your inner feelings, it is obviously a sign that either this is not the teacher for you or maybe that you are not ready for that teacher, while you may be in the future.

If you spend time with a teacher, verify that what he or she teaches is beneficial and that students have had good experiences. It is always good to remain vigilant and compare modern teachings to the original, authentic teachings. Teachings should always be derived from some ancient texts or other validated sources, as true spiritual teachings have always been brought to the world by enlightened beings and not average, ego-driven people. Use your common sense when comparing the teachings of yore and a modern teacher's teachings, recalling that Tantra is derived from the ancient scriptures called *agamas*.

For many, the ego is impressed with both internal and external factors. Try to be honest with yourself. Can you honestly admit, "I'm an impressionable person and I tend to be superficial"? If you tend to be such a person, you should make a point of writing down the advantages or skills of a teacher you've met. In addition, it would be helpful to make a list of pros and cons for that teacher and examine whether these describe the person internally and genuinely or on the basis of hearsay, gossip, reputation, and social pressure. Not every famous teacher is an authentic spiritual person. From your list of pros and cons, consider whether your reasoning is more internal or intuitive. For example, ask yourself, when I hear him talking, does it make sense? Is there an intrinsic logic to what he says? Personally I had done my own studies of yogic texts before I met my guru so when he spoke I knew that it fit, that it was the inspirational voice of a yogi spirit. If your quest is in Buddhism, search the *Dhammapada* so you get the spirit and already understand who you seek in terms of essence. Then you have a better means of evaluating.

Not every teacher fits every student. Sometimes a teacher may be a very good teacher but he or she doesn't fit you personally. Even if a teacher is an authentic teacher, be aware that you should also choose a teacher who fits your personal style and temperament. It is also the case that you may find a good teacher, but the timing may not be right and your relationship also will not fit as a result. Generally, have patience. Give your search some time. Study, practice, and see whether you yourself are evolving with the teachings of a teacher.

> *If you are irritated by every rub,*
> *how will your mirror be polished?*
> — Rumi

The guru's wish is your well-being and evolution. In a tantric environment the guru is a very integral part of the lifestyle. He or she will be present at big events, in meditation, at initiations, and in various other situations. He will help you to progress carefully and safely in your evolution as you navigate common obstacles along the way, which may be very challenging or misleading unless the guru is there presiding with lucidity in the situation. The lucidity of the guru is called *viveka*, which means discrimination in Sanskrit. With the ability to discriminate properly, the guru can tell you what is real and not real, whether your ego is talking or you are making a mistake. Metaphorically, it is like being led carefully along the right path as you pass through a minefield so you don't step in the wrong places.

Of course there are always some challenges that you have to face yourself, because it is your evolution ultimately. Even the ability to accept a guru and surrender to his guidance is a test, because it is common in modern times to think we know everything and to celebrate our independent spirit – that nobody "tells us what to do." But a guru's help is so valuable that the tantric texts even say that the guru is Shiva. In other words, the guru is like the hand of God there to help you progress in a harmonious way. That is how sacred and important the guru is.

XIII

CONCLUSION

A PERSONAL NOTE

As you have seen so far, Tantra is indeed a science and an art. We have explored the vast reach of Tantra and its significant promise for human sexuality.

At this point I would like to emphasize that all the tantric knowledge presented in this book exists as the confirmed actual experience of tantric masters, teachers, and practitioners who have lived throughout history and still live today. Tantra is not based in theoretical make-believe and wishful thinking; rather it is real-life knowledge based in truth that has been applied in practice and mastered by tantrics and yogis around the world, throughout the march of time, over and over like a proven experiment.

I have received all of this knowledge from a tantric master with whom I studied for years and continue to study with today – my guru, Swami Vivekananda Saraswati – and I have seen it powerfully at work in the lives of many fellow tantrics and quite a few of my own students (whose short stories are sprinkled throughout this book).

Therefore, I stress this point to reassure the reader that the information presented in this book has been tested and verified in many years of practice and is directly derived from the authentic lineages of the ancient tantric masters of India and Tibet.

One obvious question may stare the reader in the face at the conclusion of this book: How exactly can I bring Tantra into my life? This is indeed a very important question. I have seen in my many years of tantric practice and teaching that some practitioners have problems in their training and encounter difficulties when they aim to integrate Tantra into their lives – despite their hope to do this in a harmonious way and without creating challenges for themselves or their loved ones.

My first suggestion would be to undergo the transformation to a tantric lifestyle in a gradual and intelligent manner. Quick, abrupt, or aggressive changes in lifestyle can be harmful and may even take one off the tantric path instead of leading to the desired results. It is important to keep in mind that big life changes should always be approached with care and maturity, without generating resistance or antagonism within yourself or your environment.

Experience shows that, while starting out on the tantric path may be a great adventure and a spiritual revelation for many practitioners, those who know them may misunderstand the tantric lifestyle or be confused by the changes they witness in someone they know. These observers – we speak of people who know and even love us, like our friends and family or co-workers – may reflect very conventional and mainstream scrutiny upon our practice, casting doubt and even fear into tantric beginners and impeding their progress. Be aware that not everyone will be happy for your happiness, because people fear the unknown and they may feel like they are "losing" you to your new path – they are losing the you they knew who may have had a different way of life and priorities. For this reason, I always recommend that beginners keep their tantric practices private (or within couples who practice together) unless they find themselves in a tantric community where this path is understood and supported.

Furthermore, it is important not to be too obsessive or attached to specific goals. For example, some hear about the promise of multiple orgasms in Tantra (certainly one of Tantra's great gifts to practitioners) and become very goal-oriented and fixated on achieving this as soon as possible. As a result, if such orgasms don't manifest in their lives as soon as expected, they may become discouraged and disappointed and may even decide to throw in the towel. Please remember that it is important to cultivate detachment and a patient, relaxed attitude without worry. Keep in mind that what one person can do, another can achieve as well. But since we are all different – with different challenges, blockages, body structures, and destinies – it is not realistic or proper to compare ourselves to others and, in this way, to develop unrealistic expectations.

Take your time and, most importantly, enjoy the process itself. It is a great journey and can be very fulfilling for yourself and your partner.

Another obstacle worth mentioning here is related to the male orgasm itself. The shift from the short, explosive ejaculatory orgasm to a deep, tantric multiple or extended orgasm is not always easy for men. In my experience, I can definitely say that many men struggle on this point. We need to remember that this change takes some time and depends heavily on one's overall lifestyle, diet, level of purification of body, mind, and energy, and – most of all – on the development of sensitivity. Many men find this concept of sensitivity difficult to grasp and they expect the tantric orgasm to be similar to the explosive orgasms they grew accustomed to over years or decades. Here I would advise men that, as we spent years "practicing" the explosive orgasm, we need to keep in mind that the tantric orgasm must be developed. It is a new skill. I would equate it with learning how to build a fire. To build a fire, you cannot begin by throwing in the big logs and expecting the fire to blaze up quickly. It never works this way. You need to learn to use kindling, maybe some leaves or newspaper, teasing the embers into flames with smaller pieces of wood, then small logs ... allowing the fire to build up slowly into a strong blaze. At that point, you can throw in any big log and the fire will remain robust and enduring.

In the same way, in the beginning, as a man is learning to orgasm in the tantric style, I would advise that he pay attention to the small, tingly pleasures that arise. While it may be true that at this point they are not as impressive as the quick, explosive orgasm he was used to previously (and that is why some men get discouraged at this point and leave Tantra), remember that this is the beginning! As you focus your attention on the pleasurable little tingles that come, notice how with experience and more attention, they begin to slowly grow into small waves of lovely energy and pleasure. As you continue your practice, the waves increase and the pleasure grows even more until you reach a fully orgasmic stage of amazing pleasure that can last for a long time. Try to remain aware that this process will take time and is different for each man. Patience and faith in the practice are invaluable to one's development and success during this process.

THE ESSENCE OF LIFE

In the millennia of human history, we find that the search for happiness, bliss, and life's purpose has led human beings in so many directions, sexuality being one of the most common of those directions. For thousands of years human beings looked for ways to make the sexual act more satisfying, powerful, intimate, ecstatic, and meaningful. From the *Kama Sutra* and Tantra of India to Imsak in the Middle East and sexual Tao in China, humans have made every effort possible to reach that blissful essence of life with the use of various techniques, aphrodisiacs, potions, and herbs. The sexual union from which all life springs is meaningful to every aspect of our lives, bringing us ultimately to our essence and source. Consequently, tantric knowledge and teachings are priceless and should be studied seriously by anyone who wishes to discover this essence and enact real transformation in their lives.

Many times throughout my years of teaching Tantra workshops I have been asked the same question by students: "Why isn't this knowledge being taught in schools?" Or they have lamented, "I wish I would have learned about this a long time ago!" Well, this book aims to correct these oversights and help those who aspire to courageously walk the path of Tantra.

I hope that you are inspired to embark on this path and, to you, I offer my most sincere wish that you experience success and divine grace in your tantric practice. And in humbleness for all that has been offered to me through Tantra, I end on this note of gratitude to the supreme guru: Blessed be Shiva....

GLOSSARY

Abhinavagupta: Renowned Kashmiri scholar, aesthetician, mystic, musician, and poet, Abhinavagupta (950-1020) also completed more than 35 works in his life, of which the most well known is the *Tantraloka*, a fundamental treatise of Kashmiri Shaivist monistic philosophy.

agamas: Defined as "that which has come to us," the *agamas* are the ancient texts that form the basis of Tantra. Classified as *Vaishnava* and *Saiva* texts, the *agamas* expounded on a number of subjects including Yoga, *mantras*, and spiritual philosophy, and provided guidelines for them.

ajna **chakra:** The sixth chakra, *ajna* is often called the "third eye," linked with intelligence, mental clarity, telepathy, and powers of the mind, and overseeing all chakras below this point in the human being.

anahata **chakra:** The fourth chakra, meaning "unstruck," is the seat of the heart – unconditional love, affectivity of the emotions, empathy, selflessness, and devotion. *Anahata* is associated with the air element.

asanas: The physical postures of *Hatha Yoga, asanas* bring us into attunement with various energies of the universe through resonance on the chakras of the human being.

brahmacharya: One of the *yamas* of Yoga, and advised for all spiritual aspirants, brahmacharya means "sexual continence," or the retention of *ojas*, the life force. *Brahmacharya* is mainly achieved through celibacy or Tantric / Taoist practices.

chakras: Centers of force in the human being, placed slightly outside seven vital points and representing planes of consciousness and "resonance portals" with the energies of the universe.

devadasi: These temple dancers were tantric practitioners who embodied the Goddess through sacred dance and tantric arts.

Hatha Yoga: Literally "Sun-Moon" Yoga, this is the physical practice of Yoga using *asanas* to balance the lunar and solar energies in the human body.

kalas: A mysterious fluid emitted from a woman, especially during G-spot orgasm. Tantrics believe this fluid is the materialization of an exceptional form of energy.

Kali Yuga: The current cosmic era in which we live, correlated with the "Iron Age" of human history, this is the last and most spiritually debased cosmic cycle, during which time spiritual efforts are more difficult. When this *yuga* concludes, the cycle of *yugas* will continue, bringing another "Golden Age"... and eventually another Iron Age.

Karma Yoga: Known as the "path of action," this is the branch of Yoga advocated by Krishna in the *Bhagavad-Gita* – consecrated action in which the "fruits," or results, of an action are renounced and dedicated to God so that karma is not accumulated in the process of the action.

Kinsey, Dr. Alfred: An American biologist, zoologist, and sexologist (1894-1956), Kinsey was best known for his reports on male and female sexual behavior in the early 1950s. A polyamorous and bisexual married man, his research and methods were at times controversial.

Kriya Yoga: The form of Yoga described in the *Hatha Yoga Pradipika* involving six methods of purification. This may also be used to refer to other styles of Yoga intended primarily to purify the body or mind.

kundalini: Coiled three and a half times in *muladhara* chakra, near the perineum, the massive "serpent power" energy – when activated – rises through the spine to unite with consciousness in *sahasrara*. If the body does not have the purity necessary for unimpeded energetic flow, this process can be difficult, uncomfortable, or dangerous.

Kundalini Yoga: An energetic style of Yoga meant to activate the *kundalini* force in the body.

lingam: The tantric name for the male phallus, representing the supreme masculine force in the universe, Shiva.

Maha Vidyas: The tantric Cosmic Powers, or goddesses, the *Maha Vidyas* represent the 10 faces of Shakti, each with her own special energy and resonance.

maithuna: A tantric lovemaking ritual involving use of items which represent the five elements.

manipura **chakra:** The third chakra in the human being, situated just below the navel, this is the seat of courage, willpower, confidence, and inner harmony. *Manipura* is associated with the fire element.

mantras: Sounds, syllables, words, or even long phrases (most often in Sanskrit) which represent the energy of something – a goddess, chakra, etc. *Mantras* need to be transmitted by initiation in person to become fixed in the aura of a person.

Milarepa: Tibet's most famous yogi, Milarepa (1052-1135) was a black magician and murderer before turning to his guru, Marpa, and a life of austerities and yogic practices, which eventually led to his enlightenment.

mudras: Putting any part of the body (hands, sphincters, inner control at certain levels of the being, etc.) into a certain position to generate a factor of resonance or a certain result. For example, the mudra in which we hold the fingers or hands during meditation will influence the nature of that meditation.

muladhara chakra: The first chakra in the human being, *muladhara* represents the root chakra, the seat of vitality and strength and home of the latent *kundalini* force. *Muladhara* is associated with the earth element.

nirvana: Literally "to be extinguished," *nirvana* is known as the liberation from suffering and *samsara*, illusion, in Buddhist teachings – or in other words, enlightenment.

niyama: As described by Patanjali, the five *niyamas* represent the "shall-dos" of Yoga: cleanliness, contentment, austerity, self-study, and surrender to God. They form the moral imperatives of Raja Yoga paired with the *yamas*, the restraints of Yoga.

ojas: The finite life force in the human being, which is responsible for creative genius, spiritual aspiration, sexual desire and potency, etc. Each person's *ojas* is squandered beginning at birth through stress, sports, exertion, childbirth, and ejaculation, among other things.

prakriti: In *Sankhiya* and Kashmiri Shaivist philosophy, *prakriti* represents Shakti, energy, or all of manifestation.

prana: The life force of the human being, plants, animals, and nature, also referred to as *chi* and *ki* in the Chinese and Japanese traditions, respectively.

pranayama: Techniques and methods used to obtain control of the *prana* within the human body, most often focusing on control of the breath and specific breath rhythming.

purusha: In *Sankhiya* and Kashmiri Shaivist philosophy, *purusha* represents the unmanifested, or consciousness.

sadhana: Any earnest tantric or yogic practice, approached with discipline to reach an ego-transcending spiritual goal.

sahasrara **chakra:** The seventh center of consciousness, located at the crown of the human being, denotes lucidity, detachment, and enlightened wisdom.

samadhi: The state of oneness and cosmic union with God reached through any of various yogic, tantric, and meditative practices.

samyama: A yogic practice of identification used to reach a profound understanding of another being or state of consciousness.

Sankhiya: A dualistic philosophical system regarded as one of the oldest in India, *Sankhiya (or Sankhya)* forms the basis for Tantra. It states that the universe can be known by its division into *prakriti* (Shakti or manifestation) and *purusha* (Shiva or consciousness), with the *jiva* or *jivatman*, the individual spark of divine consciousness, bound to *prakriti* by desire and freed by liberation, or *moksha*.

satori: Sudden enlightenment representing the goal of Zen Buddhism.

Shakti: The ultimate feminine principle representing energy and all of manifestation, she is embodied as the consort of Shiva.

Shiva: The supreme masculine force in the universe which also represents consciousness or God, the Absolute.

shivalingam: A statue or image of the conjoined *lingam* (phallus, or representation of Shiva) and *yoni* (or vagina, surrounding the *lingam* and representing Shakti) – together symbolizing the eternal cosmic union of the supreme male and female principles.

shunyata: A concept in Buddhism meaning the void, nothingness, emptiness, and leading to the concept or state of not-self.

Sivananda, Swami: A doctor who eventually gave up his practice for monastic life, Sivananda (1887-1963) was a beloved spiritual teacher who founded the Sivananda Ashram, Divine Life Society, and wrote more than 200 books on Yoga, Vedanta, and other subjects.

svadhisthana **chakra:** The second chakra, located near and just above the genitals, is associated with sexuality, imagination, creativity, and the collective subconscious. *Svadhisthana* is associated with the water element.

tapas: One of the five *niyamas, tapas* refers to austerities and yogic discipline.

vira: The supreme masculine state or hero, characterized by nobleness, courage, virtue, spiritual verticality, and honor.

virya: From the Sanskrit (and Pali), a term commonly associated with Buddhism, *virya* means energy, enthusiasm, diligence, or effort.

vishuddha **chakra:** The fifth chakra, located at the throat, is associated with divine mystery, high intelligence and aesthetics, musical composition, literary brilliance, and all things related with the cosmos. *Vishuddha* is associated with the element of ether.

viveka: From Sanskrit meaning "discrimination."

yama: As described by Patanjali, the five *yamas* represent the "shall-nots" or restraints of Yoga: non-violence, truthfulness, non-theft, non-possessiveness, and sexual continence. They form the moral imperatives of Raja Yoga paired with the *niyamas*, that which is advised and beneficial in Yoga.

yoni: The tantric name for the female vagina, representing the supreme feminine force in the universe, Shakti.

yuga: In the traditions of Yoga and Vedic lore, this is a cosmic cycle of approximately 6,400 years.

ABOUT BHAIRAVA YOGA

Bhairava Yoga is a European school of Yoga, Tantra, and meditation founded by Somananda Moses Maimon in 2010 and based in Estonia. Bhairava is a branch of the Agama Yoga School offering a year-round curriculum of Yoga teachings, a multitude of Tantra workshops, and tantric massage courses for singles and couples alike.

Bhairava Yoga is also the lead organizer of an annual International Tantra Festival in Estonia, which brings together Tantra enthusiasts, students, and teachers from around the world.

We welcome you to join any of our teachings or activities, or you may also contact us to arrange workshop teachings in your area.

Bhairava Yoga
Narva mnt 11d, Tallinn 10151, Estonia
+372 59 19 67 88
www.bhairavayoga.com
www.tantrafestival.ee
info@bhairavayoga.com

CPSIA information can be obtained
at www.ICGtesting.com
Printed in the USA
BVHW031447170822
644852BV00007B/234